The human-animal bond is as old as human history. We cherish our animal companions for their unconditional affection and acceptance. We feel a thrill when we glimpse wild creatures in their natural habitat or in our own backyard.

Unfortunately, the human-animal bond has at times been weakened. Humans have exploited some animal species to the point of extinction.

The Humane Society of the United States makes a difference in the lives of animals here at home and worldwide. The HSUS is dedicated to creating a world where our relationship with animals is guided by compassion. We seek a truly humane society in which animals are respected for their intrinsic value, and where the human-animal bond is strong.

Want to help animals? We have plenty of suggestions. Adopt a pet from a local shelter, join The Humane Society and be a part of our work to help companion animals and wildlife. You will be funding our educational, legislative, investigative and outreach projects in the U.S. and across the globe.

Or perhaps you'd like to make a memorial donation in honor of a pet, friend or relative? You can through our Kindred Spirits program. And if you'd like to contribute in a more structured way, our Planned Giving Office has suggestions about estate planning, annuities, and even gifts of stock that avoid capital gains taxes.

Maybe you have land that you would like to preserve as a lasting habitat for wildlife. Our Wildlife Land Trust can help you. Perhaps the land you want to share is a backyard— that's enough. Our Urban Wildlife Sanctuary Program will show you how to create a habitat for your wild neighbors.

So you see, it's easy to help animals. And The HSUS is here to help.

THE HUMANE SOCIETY
OF THE UNITED STATES.

2100 L Street NW • Washington, DC 20037 • 202-452-1100
www.hsus.org

The Complete

Personal Finances Online
REFERENCE

Step-by-Step Instructions to Take Control of Your Financial Future Using the Internet

By Tamsen Butler

THE COMPLETE GUIDE TO YOUR PERSONAL FINANCES ONLINE:
STEP-BY-STEP INSTRUCTIONS TO TAKE CONTROL OF YOUR
FINANCIAL FUTURE USING THE INTERNET

Copyright © 2011 Atlantic Publishing Group, Inc.
1405 SW 6th Avenue • Ocala, Florida 34471 • Phone 800-814-1132 • Fax 352-622-1875
Web site: www.atlantic-pub.com • E-mail: sales@atlantic-pub.com
SAN Number: 268-1250

Library of Congress Cataloging-in-Publication Data

Butler, Tamsen, 1974-
  The complete guide to your personal finances online : step-by-step instructions to take control of your financial future using the internet / by Tamsen Butler.
     p. cm.
  Includes bibliographical references and index.
  ISBN-13: 978-1-60138-297-9 (alk. paper)
  ISBN-10: 1-60138-297-9 (alk. paper)
 1. Internet banking. 2. Home banking services. 3. Banks and banking--Automation. 4. Electronic funds transfers--Security measures. 5. Finance, Personal. I. Title.
  HG1708.7.B88 2010
  332.02400285'4678--dc22
                              2010028228

All trademarks, trade names, or logos mentioned or used are the property of their respective owners and are used only to directly describe the products being provided. Every effort has been made to properly capitalize, punctuate, identify, and attribute trademarks and trade names to their respective owners, including the use of ® and ™ wherever possible and practical. Atlantic Publishing Group, Inc. is not a partner, affiliate, or licensee with the holders of said trademarks.

LIMIT OF LIABILITY/DISCLAIMER OF WARRANTY: The publisher and the author make no representations or warranties with respect to the accuracy or completeness of the contents of this work and specifically disclaim all warranties, including without limitation warranties of fitness for a particular purpose. No warranty may be created or extended by sales or promotional materials. The advice and strategies contained herein may not be suitable for every situation. This work is sold with the understanding that the publisher is not engaged in rendering legal, accounting, or other professional services. If professional assistance is required, the services of a competent professional should be sought. Neither the publisher nor the author shall be liable for damages arising herefrom. The fact that an organization or Web site is referred to in this work as a citation and/or a potential source of further information does not mean that the author or the publisher endorses the information the organization or Web site may provide or recommendations it may make. Further, readers should be aware that Internet Web sites lis Printed on Recycled Paper work may have changed or disappeared between when this work was written and when it i

Printed in the United States

PROJECT MANAGER: Melissa Peterson
PEER REVIEWER: Marilee Griffin • mgriffin@atlantic-pub.com
COVER DESIGN: Jackie Miller • millerjackiej@gmail.com

AUTHOR DEDICATION

Thanks to my personal cheerleading squad: Scott, the Lincolns, Ashley Aisenson, and my dear sister Laurie, who is the only person who squeals in delight each time I have a book published.

A special thank you to the Kippers for keeping me stocked with coffee and to the coffee houses in Papillion for the office space.

Finally, thanks to Melissa Peterson at Atlantic Publishing for sticking with me through three books and countless deadline extensions.

TABLE OF CONTENTS

FOREWORD   13

INTRODUCTION   17

My Story 18

Why Should I Switch to Online Banking? 19

Inside this Book 21

CHAPTER 1: What the Internet Can Do for You 23

The Pros and Cons of Online Financial Management 25

It is Easier than You Think 28

Personal Finances 101 30

The Importance of Keeping Track of Your Money...32

The Importance of Accessibility 34

Checklist: Do You Have These Accounts? 36

CHAPTER 2: Getting Ready: Software and Safety 41

Using Personal Finance Software to Manage Your Money...42

Installing Money Management Software Safely 47

Crafting the Perfect Password..............................51

Public Computer Usage.......................................55

Antivirus, Spyware, and Firewall Software 57

Computer Maintenance 101 65

Meeting System Requirements 66

Using an Effective Internet Connection.................69

Installing a Printer 70

Backing Up Important Information to an
External Source 71

Staying Organized 73

Ready to Go! 76

CHAPTER 3: Making the Switch to Online Banking 79

Making the Move...80

Online Banking Feature Must-Haves....................90

Nice Perks for Online Banking Features 95

Electronic Communication 98

Online Banking Security Features......................100

Account Management and Monitoring 103

Online Account Transfers...................................108

Online Deposits..115

Ordering Replacements 120

Need Help?...123

CHAPTER 4: Online Bill Paying 127

Get Started 128

CHAPTER 5: Online Money Management 137

Online Budget Tools 138

Online Spending Logs 145

Online Asset Management 149

CHAPTER 6: Borrowing Money Online 157

Online Comparison "Shopping" 159

Applying for Credit 162

Estimate Debt Payments 176

CHAPTER 7: Online Shopping & Saving Money 183

Comparison Shopping 183

Coupons and More 185

Online Auctions 189

Shopping Online Safely 192

PayPal 194

CHAPTER 8: Online Investing 197

Before Investing 199

Start Investing Online 200

Maintaining Your Online Investment Account.....205

Seasoned Investors 213

The Top 10 Online Investment Mistakes.............216

CHAPTER 9: Managing Long-term Savings   221

Your Retirement Accounts...................................222

College Savings Accounts 226

CHAPTER 10: Managing Your Benefits   231

Health Care Coverage...233

Retirement Funds 235

Your Paycheck 236

Social Security 238

CHAPTER 11: Managing Taxes Online   241

Online Resources 242

Estimating Taxes Online 245

CHAPTER 12: Personal Property Management   249

Home Inventory...249

Insurance 253

Market Values...257

CHAPTER 13: Online Financial Education   261

Who Can You Trust? 262

CONCLUSION: Your Finances Will Thank You   269

APPENDIX: List of Helpful Websites   271

BIBLIOGRAPHY   279

AUTHOR BIOGRAPHY   281

INDEX   283

years, we are finally seeing a transition to a semi-paperless society. I do not expect we ever will go 100 percent paperless, but any amount would be better than none.

Many CPA firms now receive documents electronically to prepare tax returns. Once the tax returns are prepared, they then give their clients copies of the tax returns in digital format. Investment companies are another example. Many of them now offer the majority of their documents in digital format, which can easily be e-mailed or downloaded from the Web.

As companies develop this technology, it allows individuals to access data or prepare documents in digital format versus paper format. The best part is that it is easier than you might imagine, and you are helping Mother Earth while you are at it. Why do I say easier? Let us think about it for a moment. It is much easier to fire up your computer and look for a file versus going to the basement and looking through drawers or boxes, hoping you will find the papers where you stored them — or where you thought you stored them. Once you have gone paperless, you no longer need to worry about losing all of your personal documents to a flooded basement or too much humidity. On top of that, you have fewer boxes to move to your next house.

even though this book does not have the word "paperless" in the title, it ry well could. Because so many companies and individuals are going erless, this book is a very timely must-read. Author Tamsen Butler has ided more than enough detail to help you accomplish a task online, still keeping it simple enough to avoid frustration.

better to write a book about using technology to manage your fi-
online than someone who was practically forced to do it? After
oversees, Butler was required to make a choice: either stick to the

FOREWORD

In the 1980s, the personal computer became more affordable and c
puter processing speeds increased — nothing like today's speed, but
faster than the older technology. The buzzword in technology cir
"paperless." Paperless occurs when documents are saved in digit
on computers or remote locations. To many people, going pape
mean no more cutting of trees. At that time, it also was com
people say, "Personal computers are going to put the print
out of business!" But, it still has not completely happened

As a working CPA and financial adviser, I now hear th
happened to the paperless society?" This question gen
ents who have to sign abundant investment docume
notice the numerous pages on which their tax retu

old way of communicating, which sometimes took days or weeks (no offense to the good people with the U.S. Postal Service), or to simply turn on her computer and access information instantly. In this book, she has turned her own personal learning experiences into a simple "how-to" book for you. Many people think online finance means paying bills online or online banking, but as you read her book, you will quickly find that there are many other everyday things that the Internet can be used for.

Even though the title of the book is "Step-by-Step Instructions to Take Control of Your Financial Future Using the Internet," she does a wonderful job of explaining much of the financial terminology with what she calls "Learn the Lingo" sections. She does it in a simple way, making it easy to understand and without intimidation, targeting the average person who wants to learn how to do things online. She has written the book from personal experience and without the assumption that you know too much or too little. Personally, I have read many financial books with too much unexplained technical lingo. I would be willing to bet many people never finish reading those types of books. People who do finish the books often end up being more confused than when they started. As a CPA and financial adviser, I educate others about finances and taxes. While reading the book, even I found some new and very useful things that I did not know existed on the Web.

There is something for everyone in this book, from individuals who are very savvy with computers and finances — probably less than 10 percent of population — to individuals who are not quite as computer-savvy — the other 90 percent. However, if you are one of the latter individuals, you, especially, will find the book very helpful. It is a great tool that makes surfing the Web a cinch. If you read and follow Butler's method, you will avoid the usual frustrations we often run into on the Web.

John Azodi, CPA

John Azodi, CPA, is the owner and president of Azodi CPA & Investments, PC. He started his business in 1991 as a certified public accounting firm. In 1994, he expanded the business to provide 401(k) administration services to small businesses. In 1998, he registered as a financial adviser and was licensed as an insurance agent. Since then, he has worked as an independent agent. He has taught a variety of seminars and classes on topics such as tax planning, starting and running a profitable business, and investment and retirement planning.

He is author of the book *Roth IRA: Exploding the Myths, to convert or Not in 2010* (2nd edition), and the 3rd edition under the new name *How to Build Tax-Free Wealth*. You can visit his website at **www.whyrothira.com**.

Azodi is also the current host of a talk show called "Wealth is a Choice" every Saturday morning on KCMO Talk Radio 710. His show runs from 7 a.m. to 8 a.m. (CST) every Saturday and covers the Kansas City metro and surrounding areas. To listen to the show online, visit **www.710kcmo.com**.

INTRODUCTION

The Internet can be plenty of fun. People use the Internet for all sorts of reasons, from playing games and catching up on current events to keeping up with family and meeting new friends. If you have ever spent an afternoon clicking on various websites before suddenly realizing you have been surfing the Net for hours, you know how entertaining the Internet can be.

But there is another side to the World Wide Web; you can also use it to manage your personal finances. Better yet, you can use the Internet as a tool to manage your personal finances more effectively than you already manage them. Even if you currently spend very little time on the Internet, the steps required to manage all of your money online is not difficult at all. In fact, once you begin using online financial management tools regularly and with ease, you will likely view the Internet as one of the most useful resources for keeping track of your money — and maybe even saving some money while you are at it.

My Story

When my husband and I moved overseas for a two-year military assignment in Turkey, I was nervous about how we would manage our finances effectively. Mail took approximately two weeks to get to us, and it was a hassle to call the United States because we were restricted to 15-minute phone calls. This was not nearly enough time to call a financial institution, especially because the time zone difference meant we were calling our bank in the dead of the night. Luckily, our bank offered telephone customer service around the clock, but by the time I was able to talk to someone after being on hold, I usually only had three minutes to quickly ask my question.

Luckily for us, around the time of our move, our bank decided to implement online banking. Our Internet connection was painfully slow and generally unreliable, but even with these barriers, it was still easier than waiting for paper statements in the mail or trying to get by with restrictive phone lines. Having immediate access to our account information online made it much easier to manage our finances. No longer was it necessary to wait for a two-week-old paper statement to come in the mail to see how much money we had in our account. As a bonus, we felt a little more in touch with our lives back in the United States, even though we lived very far away.

After our experience with online banking, I was hooked. I signed up for online access to our credit card accounts, car loan, and even insurance and retirement accounts. I found a wide variety of online tools that I still use to effectively manage my family's finances today, such as financial calculators to help me estimate monthly bills or analyze our debt. I also know that if I have a financial question, I no longer need to wait on hold for a customer representative; I can easily find the answer online. I am positive that if I had to give up the Internet, one of the first things I would miss would be the always up-to-date access to my personal finances because I have grown so accustomed to the ease of use online banking provides.

Why Should I Switch to Online Banking?

Do you still pull out your paper check register and jot down purchases? Do you wait until your paper statement comes in the mail to make sure your credit card account is free of errors? With the Internet, you no longer have to wait for monthly account statements to arrive in the mail to make sure your personal finances are under control. All of your account information is available any time — day or night, weekday or weekend — as long as you have a secure, reliable Internet connection. Think of how much easier it will be to manage your finances when all the information you need is accessible all the time. When you always have access to your account information, as well as to numerous money management tools, the task of managing your personal finances is suddenly not so daunting.

Many people who only use the Internet to send e-mail or check the news might have the notion that managing finances online will be too complicated to master. There are also plenty of people who already utilize online banking but have not yet begun to manage other aspects of their finances online. No matter your experience level, with the help of this book, you will be proficient in no time.

Do you already use the Internet for some of your financial accounts? Perhaps you use the Internet to periodically review your stock portfolio, but you have yet to utilize the online banking features offered by your financial institution to manage your checking or savings accounts. If you already use the Internet for some aspects of your money management, you know the Internet can be a convenient and useful tool. Now it is time to take that knowledge a step further and incorporate the other online financial tools at your disposal. Whether you want to track your spending online, find out about the best investments using Internet sources, or learn more about any other financial management tools, this book will guide you through the steps necessary to find the most credible online sources and how to use them.

There are many safe, effective, and easy ways to manage your finances online. If you are ready to gain complete control of your finances by utilizing the Internet as a means to do so, this book will tell you everything you need to know. Managing your finances does not need to be difficult or stressful, especially when you have a powerful tool like the Internet at your fingertips.

Are you worried about Internet safety? If so, you certainly are not alone. Online security is a hot topic, and for those who do not understand the basics of computer security, the thought of risking your money can be enough to deter you from managing your finances online. With this book, you will learn everything you need to know about keeping your financial information safe online, including the basics of secure Internet connections, crafting the perfect password, and more.

Many financial management tools available online are absolutely free and easy to use. Do you want to know whether you can afford to buy a home rather than rent? Free calculators that estimate monthly mortgage payments are available online. Are you interested in finding out which financial institution is currently offering the best interest rates for savings accounts? A quick search using an online comparison tool will yield this information. This book provides you with the information you need to begin managing your personal finances online today. Once you have read the book and put the basics to use, keep the book in reach to use as a reference guide for the more advanced techniques and features of online financial management, such as online investing or market value research, which tells you how much your assets are actually worth. If you are like most people, you will begin by utilizing online account access or online bill pay and advance to buying insurance online or chatting with other investors about recent trades in an online forum. One of the great aspects of managing your finances online is that you are in charge; you decide which features and tools to utilize and what level of online management you are comfortable with. However, do not be surprised if you find yourself delighted by the options and freedom the Internet offers and want to move the majority — if not all — of your financial management to the Internet.

Inside this Book

This book includes everything you need to know about managing your personal finances online. Follow the step-by-step instructions and you will soon be managing your checking and savings accounts online, paying your bills utilizing an online bill pay method, managing your investments online, and using the Internet as a resource to get the best deal on purchases. When you have a firm understanding of what your money is doing and you have an easy way to tell your money what to do, you may find that you actually have more money than you thought.

Do you know where you spend the majority of your money? Online financial management allows you to see how you spend your money without tediously keeping paper records every single month. By taking control of your money and monitoring your spending habits, you will have an easier time preventing financial mistakes and making smart choices in the future.

Throughout the book, you will find case studies from people just like you who wanted to learn more about managing their finances online. Some of the people featured are completely managing their finances online, while others are still in the process of learning, but the same thing remains true for everyone featured within this book: They had to start from the beginning, just like everyone else. You will also hear from financial and Internet professionals who share their expertise to help you navigate managing your finances online. If you have a question about a particular term used throughout the book, look for the definition in one of the Learn the Lingo sidebars.

Use this book as an ongoing resource. Incorporate the things you learn when you are ready. For example, you might be anxious to get started with managing your investments online but not quite ready to handle balancing your checkbook using the Internet. When you are ready to take another step, refer back to this book for all the information you need to get started. Of course, if you want to get the full benefits of this book and all the financial management tools the Internet has to offer, you will read the book as a step-by-step guide that will ease you into managing your money online. Follow the simple steps to make the transition, and by the time you finish the book, you will have successfully made the switch to online financial management.

CHAPTER 1

WHAT THE INTERNET CAN DO FOR YOU

The Internet offers a wide variety of tools that can be used to manage your finances. Instead of waiting until you receive your bank statements at the end of the month to review transactions and balance your checkbook, online account access allows you to see when debits and credits have been posted to your account — sometimes within minutes of purchasing an item or making a deposit — without having to step foot into your financial institution. Managing your money becomes easier when it is not necessary to wait until the end of the month to see which checks have cleared and how much money is in your bank account. Most financial experts agree that a proactive approach to personal finances is key to managing your money successfully. Beyond accessing your checking and savings accounts, online money management can also include:

- Managing your credit accounts online, including credit cards and loans
- Moving money from one account or institution to another
- Paying your bills without writing a check
- Planning and managing your budget
- Researching the best financial deals
- Estimating potential payments for new loans
- Opening and managing investments online
- Estimating and filing taxes

This is not an exhaustive list. As the Internet continues to evolve, so will the resources available.

Some people are wary of the Internet in general, while others are apprehensive about the specific idea of using the Internet as a tool for financial management. They wonder whether their personal information is safe from people intending to do harm or worry that trusting online tools to manage recurring tasks — like making loan payments — will result in a loss of personal control over how their money is being handled. They wonder whether the Internet is reliable and, if not, the amount of harm that can be done as a result of a payment not getting to the creditor on time or someone stealing their credit card number online. Although these concerns have some validity in certain situations, overall, online banking and other online financial tools are quite safe and completely manageable. If you have concerns similar to these, this book intends to ease some of your worries. You will learn more about Internet security and how managing your finances online actually gives you more control over your money — not less.

The Pros and Cons of Online Financial Management

No system of money management is without flaws; although, there are certainly some methods that are better than others. Keep in mind that the potential pros and cons of managing your finances online depend largely on how you utilize the Internet and what services your preferred financial institutions offer through their websites. The pros and cons include:

- **Pro: Easy access**. With online account access, you can review your transactions any time. This can be incredibly helpful when you are trying to remember how much you spent on a specific purchase or if you need to know whether a creditor received your payment on time. This can also be a great way to immediately spot any problems that need to be addressed, such as errors on the account. This immediate access will also decrease the odds of identity theft going unnoticed. By regularly accessing your account online, you have the ability to quickly discover transactions posted to your account made as a result of a lost or stolen card or check.

- **Con: Delays to posting**. Not all transactions instantaneously appear within the online account information on your bank's website, so it is important to still take the time to review monthly transactions to make sure everything is correct. For example, some merchants who preauthorize transactions will temporarily list a transaction for the amount of the preauthorization, not of the actual purchase. These transactions often appear as "pending" in your online account information. It can take a day or two before the preauthorization amount is replaced by the actual purchase amount within the online transaction register. This is common practice among merchants who expect a tip, such as with restaurants or spas. Paying at the pump at a gas station will also result in a preauthorization, as the total amount spent will not be determined until after you have finished pumping your gas.

- **Pro: Ease of use**. Many online financial management options are automated, and you actually do very little to merge your financial records together. For example, some online budgeting tools will import information directly from your bank accounts by contacting your financial institution remotely. Paper documentation and entering account information in manually is a thing of the past. For people who have file upon file of account information gathering dust on their desks at home, this can be a huge improvement.

- **Con: Barrage of information**. When logging in to your account online, whether it is a deposit account or a revolving line of credit, you will likely have to click through at least one advertisement from your financial institution. Though this is not necessary a tedious task, as most advertised offers can quickly be declined by clicking a "No Thanks" button, the constant barrage of offers can become annoying.

- **Pro: Wide availability**. You do not have to be home in order to access the Internet. Libraries, merchants, cafés, and some cell phones offer Internet access. If you are visiting family in another state for an extended period, you can still easily manage your finances by using a family member's computer, as long as the computer you use has a secure connection.

- **Con: Potential security problems**. Not all computers are secure. In fact, your home computer may be infected with spyware that records your account information or other information you input regarding your financial situation — including your credit card number. In some cases, it is possible for computer hackers to use this information to access your financial accounts. Luckily, this situation is generally avoidable by using secure Internet connections and maintaining up-to-date virus and spyware software. *You will learn more about online security issues in Chapter 2.*

Managing your finances online also means you get to choose your level of involvement. Perhaps you are comfortable managing your deposit accounts online, but you prefer to manage your investment accounts in person with a financial adviser. With online finance management, it is not necessary to have an all-or-nothing approach; it is up to you to decide your comfort level. Once you master one form of online financial management, you may be ready to try another. Take your time and do not feel pressured to do anything you do not understand. Managing your finances is a personal endeavor, and only you can decide which features and tools are right for you and your situation.

CASE STUDY: PAYING BILLS MADE EASY
Emily, social worker

I was always very hesitant to do online bill pay. I thought I had more control over things when I wrote checks, put them in the envelope, etc. I finally got tired of the checks, stamps, and paper cuts. When I switched banks recently, I signed up for online bill pay. I wish I would have started it a long time ago. It is so easy and does not take much time at all. I still feel I have control when paying my bills. It only takes about five minutes to pay all my bills, whereas it used to take me about an hour. I will never go back to the paper method of bill paying.

> I also manage my bank accounts online. It is so nice to be able to login any time day or night, check my balance, and see which payments and credits have been processed.

It is Easier than You Think

Depending on how many financial accounts you have and how long you have been managing your finances using traditional methods, the move to online financial management may be simple or it may seem downright tedious. This can be especially true if you already have a meticulous system in place for recording your financial information. For example, if you have a carefully maintained filing cabinet of account statements dating back a few years as well as a checkbook register you loyally update every time you make a purchase using a check or debit card, you may feel especially apprehensive about making the move online. After all, if you already have a great system in place, why switch?

You will soon find that managing your finances online allows you to control your money more efficiently than you did with your cabinet full of folders and your meticulous check register, and you will also save yourself a lot of time and effort. So, though you should not feel as though you have to shred all the files you have in your cabinet or toss your check register into the trash right away, do not be surprised to realize you might not necessarily need these items at your desk after all.

It is completely understandable to be apprehensive about making the transition to managing your finances online, especially if you have little experience using a computer or accessing the Internet. This can be especially true for people who are of an older generation who did not grow up using computers and relying on the Internet for information and socialization as today's young adults have.

Or, you may be among the large group of people who have only dabbled with using the Internet and often find the process to be relatively frustrating. You are the sort of person who uses the Internet for very specific purposes: to e-mail your children who live in a different state, make online purchases here and there, or perhaps check your bank account balance once in a while — even though the process makes you a bit nervous. If using the Internet usually only results in a headache, the good news is that the Internet is constantly being improved, and you will find it less frustrating the more you use it. Financial institutions regularly review their online account management options and make changes based on research and customer feedback to better suit their users. For this reason, you can rest assured that if you made your first attempt at banking online a few years ago and found the process incredibly frustrating, there is a good chance you will have a much better experience on your next attempt.

Whether this is your first attempt at online money management or you are giving it another shot, the way in which you currently manage your finances is likely to be a process you have used for many years. You are already comfortable with "traditional" means of balancing your checkbook and paying your bills. Why do you need to learn something new? Is it worth your time to learn a new way of controlling your money?

Yes, it definitely is. You are probably thinking, "The way I manage my money has worked for years." Though this may be true, you should know that managing your money online offers a better solution. And, best of all, it is not as difficult as you think it might be.

The fact is that online financial management can make good financial management habits even better. You will save time by having the ability to pay your bills online, be able to review account information when it is convenient for you, and perhaps automate a few financial tasks — like transferring money to your savings account each month.

Most online money-management tools offer tutorials that walk you through using the tools provided by the program. If you still have trouble navigating programs or websites, most companies offer technical support personnel who are available by telephone, via e-mail, or through an online chat function that allows you to talk online in real time so you do not have to wait for the answers you need.

The Internet is designed for a wide variety of users. Whether you have virtually no experience with the Internet or you are a seasoned veteran of e-mail and social networking, do not feel intimidated by the Internet as a money management tool. The bottom line is this: Once you have all the information you need, managing your finances online really is easy.

Personal Finances 101

Chances are, you are already familiar with the basics of personal finance. You might already know about managing your money, but have yet to venture into making the switch to managing your money using online tools. Whether you have managed your finances for many years or have recently taken control of your own money for the first time, you will find that the Internet provides an easy-to-use method for financial management that accentuates and simplifies how you handle your money.

"Personal finance" refers to almost anything that relates to your money and how you spend it. This can include deposit accounts, credit accounts, insurance, investments, mortgages, or anything else pertaining to how you spend or save your money. How does the Internet make managing your personal finances easier? Not only are you able to easily monitor your money, but there are many tools online to help you stretch your money further. Beyond managing the money you already have, the Internet can be used as a resource for saving and making even more money. You can use the tools available online to carefully track your spending, investments, and savings in order to determine if you are doing what you should be doing with your money; if you are not, then you can use the same tools to help you figure out what you should actually be doing to improve your personal financial situation.

CASE STUDY: TRACKING WHAT YOU SPEND

Curt Andringa, Senior
financial manager

Do not be afraid of managing your money online. Start today. You cannot manage or control what you do not track. I feel strongly that everyone should track what they spend. If you do not know within approximately $5 what you spent on groceries last month, you probably are not being as careful with your money as you should. The best way I have found to do this is with Quicken® or a comparable program available online. Tracking finances electronically allows you to do things such as reporting, market updates, and budgeting in a couple clicks.

If you are still managing your money with a checkbook ledger and piece of paper, you also probably are not being as careful with your money as you should. In this financial environment we live in today, it is much easier to attain wealth by controlling spending than it is to increase income.

Using the online access to my accounts, I have found cases where my credit card was not billed at a store or restaurant, most likely due to an error on the store's part. This is a nice little piece of information you would not normally discover if you did not bother to track your expenses. Bank errors are rare in today's financial world; you are better off hoping to find a $20 bill laying under your couch cushion than getting a bank error in your favor.

Buying investments is all about knowledge, and the Internet offers many ways to obtain the knowledge you need to make investment decisions. Begin to watch how a stock behaves by picking one. It can be almost any stock. You will soon discover peaks and valleys and eventually be comfortable knowing when might be a good time to buy. Of course, life can always throw you a financial curve ball, so be sure you are comfortable with the amount of money you invest and know the potential risks.

You can log your investments into Microsoft Money and it will automatically update the value of your stocks or mutual funds based on that day's prices. Beyond Quicken, there are several quality financial sites depending on the features you need. For the average investor, a site like Yahoo! Finance will do the trick for all the investment news the person needs. Almost every major news site has some sort of financial page with updates on what is happening in the world of finance.

The Importance of Keeping Track of Your Money

Manage your finances effectively by regularly reviewing your accounts or periodically checking whether better interest rates are available for your deposit and credit accounts and you will have a better idea of what you need to change to make better use of your money. After all, if you do not realize that daily habits — such as stopping for a mocha latte on your way to work each morning — add up to a lot of money each month, how will you know you need to make a change? Once you take a hard look at where you spend your money, the changes you need to make may become obvious.

Some money management programs offered online tell you how much money you spent in particular categories, presenting you with graphs and charts that report what percentage of your money is spent on groceries, entertainment, gas, and other expenses. Think of how long it would take to compile all this information if you were tracking it all with a pencil and notebook. Instead, with the use of online tools, this process becomes almost instantaneous.

Though tracking your spending is not the only aspect of online financial management, it is one of the most important.

Deposit accounts

Monitoring your spending in your deposit accounts — such as checking and savings accounts — will reveal the categories in which spending may be out of control. Close monitoring of your deposit accounts will also alert you to errors made by stores or your financial institution or if your balance drops near or below zero, which can certainly be an important thing to know before you whip out your debit card to make an impulse purchase. You can also use online access to make sure payments have been debited from the account or paychecks have been direct deposited.

Credit accounts

Do you know what interest rate you are currently paying on all your credit cards and loan products? With online access, finding this information is as easy as logging into your account. You can also make sure unauthorized transactions have not been charge to your credit accounts and make payments online. Additionally, some creditors offer special incentives to customers who are willing to conduct all their business online, such as offering lower interest rates or fewer fees. You may also be able to apply for a higher credit limit or process other requests online that previously had to be accomplished in person.

CASE STUDY: WHY I AM A ONLINE BANKING FAN

Rae, military wife

I am a fan of online banking. I have not stepped foot in my bank in more than six years. I pay all of my bills online and can deposit checks via my Apple® iPhone. I think it is great to be able to pay my bills while I am away from home, plus I do not have to pay for stamps and checks to make the payments. I also like being able to log in to my account to check whether my direct deposited paycheck has been credited.

Online banking also allows my spouse to check on our finances while he is on military deployment. In addition to him being able to log in to our bank's website, we use Mint.com (**www.mint.com**), so he can get an overview of how our accounts are doing, and we do not have to waste our limited conversation time discussing our finances

The Importance of Accessibility

Have you ever allowed your personal finances to slip a little? Everyone has. Perhaps you went on vacation and forgot to take your check register along and before you knew it, you had no idea how much money was in your checking account. In this situation, some people wind up bouncing checks or paying expensive overdraft fees. It can take some time to recover from a momentary financial issue, especially if you are waiting for a paper account statement to show up in the mail to determine where your account stands.

Account accessibility can also help prevent identity theft, which involves someone gaining access to your credit card account or other personal financial information and making fraudulent purchases or using your name and good credit rating to obtain other forms of credit. If the fraud detection department of your credit card company does not catch the unusual spending and you do not have online access to your credit card account transactions, it may take you quite some time before you figure out that someone has gone on a shopping spree with your credit card number. You might not realize someone else has used your account until you try to use the card for a purchase and your credit card company declines the transaction because the card's spending limit has been maxed out by the person who stole your information. In fact, according to a 2009 report by Javelin Strategy & Research, the time it takes for an individual consumer to realize and report credit card fraud is steadily increasing. The good news is that the same report also reveals that consumer liability is usually $0 thanks to the zero liability policies in place with many credit card companies.

Though you may not be financially responsible for fraudulent purchases made on your credit card, the more transactions that occur without your consent, the more complicated it may be to recover after the theft. The sooner you realize someone has stolen your financial information, the better. For every purchase the thief made with your card, the more time you will have to spend on the phone with your creditors and the more documentation you will need to send to restore your credit card account to what it once was. By using the Internet to regularly review your account information, you can discover problems before they get out of control.

Not all instances of account problems are so dramatic. It might instead be as simple as mailing a deposit to your bank or credit union that never actually makes it into your account, yet you assumed it did, so you make purchases from the account and wind up overdrawing your account. Unless you use the Internet to monitor whether your check was deposited, you might not know your account has slipped into a negative balance. Most financial institutions charge high fees for returned checks and negative balances, so this can be a very costly mistake.

The same goes for other types of personal financial accounts. If you are an avid investor who likes to manage your own accounts, the Internet can be a perfect tool to not only manage the accounts, but to research the performance of your investments and predictions of impending market sways from investment experts who post information online.

The checklist below offers a look at the different accounts you can manage online.

Checklist: Do You Have These Accounts?

There is much more to managing finances online than simply reviewing your bank accounts. If you have one of the accounts listed below, there is an excellent chance you can manage it online without even switching your financial provider.

Deposit accounts
- ☐ Checking accounts
- ☐ Savings accounts
- ☐ Money market accounts
- ☐ Certificate of deposits

Credit accounts
- ☐ Credit cards
- ☐ Car loans
- ☐ Personal loans
- ☐ Lines of credit

Monthly Expenses
- ☐ Utility bills
- ☐ Cell phone bills

☐ Cable/Internet bill
☐ Any additional recurring monthly expenses

Mortgage accounts
☐ Primary mortgages
☐ Equity loans
☐ Equity lines of credit
☐ Escrow accounts

Retirement accounts
☐ Individual retirement accounts (IRA)
☐ 401(k)
☐ Thrift savings plans

Investment accounts
☐ Individual investment accounts
☐ Mutual fund accounts
☐ Brokerage accounts

Insurance accounts
☐ Car insurance
☐ Health insurance
☐ Homeowner's or renter's insurance
☐ Business or professional liability insurance
☐ Life insurance
☐ Any additional policies

Managing finances used to involve a desk filled with paperwork. If you lost information or had a question about a financial transaction that took place more than a couple of months ago, you knew you were in for an afternoon of attempting to connect with the right representative in the right department via the telephone to request the paperwork be sent to you through the mail, which could easily take a week or more. This is no longer true when you utilize the Internet to manage your personal finances. Getting your hands on the information that used to take you weeks to obtain now only takes a few moments on your home computer.

LEARN THE LINGO

Any new online financial and computer or Internet terms you might not already be familiar with will be defined as the words arise. Do not worry if you do not know even the most basic terminology used, because this book is designed for everyone. Everything you need to know will be explained in simple terms so you do not come away from reading this book thinking to yourself, "So what did that mean?"

Before you get started with the rest of the book, here are some basic terms you will need to know in order to best benefit from the step-by-step process presented. Look for definitions of new terms as they arise throughout this book.

Chat, also instant messaging (IM): This is a feature available on some websites that allows you to type messages to someone else in real time. With a chat function, you type a question and the question appears on the other person's computer screen immediately. The other person can then type a response, which you will see as soon as the other person clicks the "enter" or "submit" button. Though this is a very popular feature on social networking websites, many financial websites offer this feature as well, allowing you to chat with a customer service representative without having to pick up a telephone, send an e-mail, or go into a local branch.

Deposit accounts: These are accounts you have with a financial institution that you use to make deposits and hold money. Examples include checking accounts and savings accounts. These accounts may or may not pay interest. Online access to these accounts is particularly beneficial and most financial institutions offer online banking for these types of accounts.

E-mail: This is an electronic letter that is sent via the Internet. Your e-mail is accessed through an e-mail account such as Google's Gmail, MSN Hotmail, Yahoo!, or another e-mail provider. E-mail is one of the many ways you can contact your financial institution online.

Revolving accounts: This is a credit account, such as a credit card or line of credit. With revolving accounts, you have an available balance you can use for purchases, and as you utilize the balance, the amount of credit available to you decreases. As you make payments, the amount of credit available increases.

Secure: An Internet connection is deemed "secure" if it is not accessible by other computer users or unauthorized computer programs. Look for a secure connection when visiting your financial institution's website. A secure connection is indicated by a padlock icon on the page, but this does not absolutely guarantee the site's security. *There will be more information regarding how to make sure your financial institution's site is secure in the next chapter.*

Statements: You receive account statements for both deposit accounts and credit accounts, whether in the mail or electronically. These statements list the transactions that occur within the statement period including withdrawals or purchases, deposits or payments, and any fees charged by the financial institution.

Transactions: These are any change made to your deposit or credit account, such as a payment made to a credit card or an automatic payment made from a checking account.

CHAPTER 2

GETTING READY: SOFTWARE AND SAFETY

You have probably heard about some of the potential problems associated with conducting financial business over the Internet. Some people wind up with their private information inadvertently in the wrong hands, which can quickly evolve into a case of identity theft. Perhaps stories like these have dissuaded you from utilizing the Internet as a financial tool because you are simply too nervous that your information will be stolen.

You can relax. You will learn everything you need to know about keeping your financial information safe on the Internet. The Internet safety lessons you will learn in this book — combined with the myriad security measures that financial institutions employ — should assure you that your money management experience will be safe. Take all of the following tips into consideration to make sure your online transactions are as secure as possible.

Using Personal Finance Software to Manage Your Money

Personal financial software, such as Quicken or the Simple Joe series (**www. simplejoe.com**) can be purchased and installed on your computer easily and can also be accentuated by the Internet. With software programs such as these, you can have your personal finance software communicate with the online access to your accounts, merging your financial management into one easy-to-handle package.

Before deciding on particular money management software, read reviews from both financial experts and consumers who have tried the software. Visit a review website to read reviews and find out about the various features offered by the software programs. A good review website is the TopTenREVIEWS' website (**www.personal-finance-software-review. toptenreviews.com**).

It is important to note that some manufacturers are beginning to move toward online money management programs, such as Mint.com (**www. mint.com**), as opposed to the type of financial management software that consumers can buy in a store and load onto their computers. For example, Microsoft Money, which was once one of the most popular money management software programs, is no longer available for purchase in stores or online unless you buy from an individual through a website such as Amazon.com or eBay. You may have Microsoft Money preloaded on your home computer, and if this is the case, you can still use it. This is likely to be a continuing trend as software manufacturers adjust to online innovations that allow consumers to manage finances over the Internet. Online money management programs, which are sometimes referred to as "in the cloud" software because they operate entirely online and information is stored on the Internet instead of on individual computers, take up less space on your computer but also leave you at the mercy of the website. In other words, if the website shuts down — either temporarily or permanently — this can affect your ability to manage your finances. Consider the pros and cons before you decide on one money management program over another.

If you do want to purchase personal finance software for your computer, here are some of the programs you have to choose from:

- **Quicken**: When browsing through available personal finance software options, this is the program you will encounter most often. There are starter and deluxe editions that offer varying features depending on the version. There are also versions of Quicken specifically intended to assist small business owners and landlords with managing expenses and income related to their businesses.

  What can you expect from the Quicken money management software? Although the actual features depend on which version of the software you buy, you can generally expect basic budgeting tools, including the creation and management of a budget. You will also be able to track your spending, balance your checking account, and get quick glances at information that may otherwise take longer to access, such as the total amount of money you have deposited into all of your accounts from various financial institutions. Quicken will also export information to some tax software programs including TurboTax, which can simplify the tax process considerably. Find out more about Quicken at **http://quicken.intuit.com** including how and where to buy the program and its functions.

- **Microsoft Money**: Although this software is no longer offered by the manufacturer, many people have this program already preloaded onto computers that were purchased prior to Microsoft discontinuing production of the software. It is also possible to buy this program from individual sellers.

Should you buy Microsoft Money? Because Microsoft has stopped selling this product, you might not be able to obtain customer support. This means that if you buy the program and then encounter problems, you might be out of luck. You may also encounter problems if you want the software to automatically update account information by importing data from your financial institution. If you simply want to create a budget and track your spending, Microsoft Money can be an option, but it probably makes more sense to go with a program such as Quicken, which will offer customer support and the option to set up automatic updates. In fact, according to Microsoft's website, after January 2011, the bill pay functions, direct online banking, and automatic software updates will no longer be available. Check Microsoft's website (**www.microsoft.com/money**) for updates about online support.

- **YNAB**: This personal finance software, which stands for "You Need a Budget," helps users create a budget and maintain the budget using the program. This software also helps users understand where money is being wasted and projects potential ways to save money overall. This software also allows data to be imported from deposit accounts as long as your financial institution provides online access to account information.

Some users feel that this program is much easier to use than other programs, but this same simplicity has prompted others to complain that the program does not offer enough options. This software may be a good option for you if your main concern is creating a budget and having a program assist you in sticking to the budget; although, it is important to note that you can find similar technology for free online. Visit the YNAB website (**www.youneedabudget.com**) for more information about the product and to download a free 7-day trial.

- **Big E-Z Books**: This software is designed to be simple and consists of spreadsheets that will track your spending as well as your income. This software is not as detailed other personal financial software that is available, and you may be able to obtain similar spreadsheets using Excel or another spreadsheet software program. If, on the other hand, you want Excel-type spreadsheets for personal financial management, but you have no interest in creating the spreadsheets yourself, this program can be an option. As with YNAB, however, you may be able to find similar tools available online free of charge. Find out more about Big E-Z Books at **www.bigez.com**.

The chart on the next page offers more information on various personal finance software programs.

These are some of the most popular personal financial management programs available, but there are many others. Which program is best for you depends on what you are looking for in financial management software. You should also consider using free online financial management websites before spending money on expensive software programs. *Online personal finances sites are discussed further in Chapter 6.*

	Quicken Starter Edition	Moneydance	AceMoney	BankTree Personal	RichOrPoor	iCash	Budget Express
Import account data	X	X	X	X		X	X
Reconcile accounts	X	X	X	X	X	X	X
Online banking	X	X	X				
Bill pay service	X	X					
Categorize & track spending	X	X	X	X	X	X	X
Write/print checks	X	X					
Find loan rates	X			X			
Personal investing reports	X	X	X	X	X	X	
Tax reports	X	X	X			X	
Loan calculator		X	X	X			X
Mortgage calculator	X	X	X	X			
Savings calculator			X				
Password protection	X	X	X	X	X	X	X
Import investment account data		X	X				
Download stock quotes		X		X			
Online manual	X	X	X	X	X	X	X
Tutorials	X	X	X	X		X	X
Phone support	X						
E-mail support	X	X	X	X	X	X	X
Live chat support	X						
Community forums	X	X	X			X	

CASE STUDY: FINDING THE
RIGHT SOFTWARE

Kyle Robberts, systems engineer,
Microsoft Certified Professional
(MCP),
Certified Ethical Hacker (CEH)

The right software is usually a matter of personal preference. Many people use Quicken, QuickBooks, or Peachtree. Whatever software you choose, be sure to research it before you try it. Many software companies allow free trial of the software before you purchase it. These can usually be downloaded from the company's website.

If you like the software, you can usually activate the trial version to make it a full functioning copy of the software. Every install will be a little different depending on which program you choose, but are all basically the same as far as the download process and features offered with the program. You will be asked questions about your name and other information to register the software. Fill in as much information as you can, and follow the on-screen instructions. Most of the procedures will involve reading the prompts and clicking next through to the next page. It is not usually a difficult process at all.

Installing money management software safely

There are many money management programs to choose from that can assist you with managing your finances. You can get your hands on these programs in a variety of ways. Some computers come preloaded with financial management software such as Quicken. You can also purchase software separately at a variety of stores and then load it onto your computer. Financial management programs are also available for download using the Internet.

You might also need to download other programs to your computer if your financial institution's online account access has features that require specific programs in order to use it. Examples include programs that integrate your account information with another program to help you track your spending or certain bill payment services. For example, some online account access programs allow you to export your account transactions over to financial management software.

If you encounter problems when installing financial management software, you can call or e-mail technical support for assistance. Most problems are easily fixed, so there is no reason to muddle through a computer problem you do not understand. Also, if you install the program incorrectly or somehow cause a problem with your computer system, you can do damage to how your computer operates overall.

LEARN THE LINGO

Direct deposit: An electronic transfer of funds from an employer's payroll account into the deposit account of an employee.

FAQ: This acronym stands for frequently asked questions. An FAQ page is offered by websites to answer routine questions commonly asked by customers. Search an FAQ page if you have a question about the usage or capabilities of the website you are using or you have questions about some of the products offered by the financial institution.

Search engine: This is a tool offered through the Internet allowing you to look for specific items. For example, if you are looking for Bank of America's official website, just type "Bank of America official website" into the search engine, which will result in possibilities presented by the search engine. You can then click on the most appropriate result to go straight to that website. Popular search engines include Google, Yahoo!, and Bing.

> **Bookmark:** This is a method available through your Internet browser that allows you to mark and save a website you visit frequently so you can access it quickly and easily next time. Bookmarks are also called "Favorites."

Keep in mind that downloading any program to your computer — whether it is a software program you purchase at a store or a program you download from the Internet — has the potential to cause harm to your computer. You likely will not have to worry about security issues if you obtain a valid copy from a legitimate company, but you should be extremely cautious with any downloadable financial management programs that come from an unfamiliar source. Avoid free financial management programs whose source cannot be verified or that you received secondhand from someone else. Free online programs are not inherently harmful, but you should download them directly from the website of the official software manufacturer. All it takes is a single download of malicious software to cause serious damage to your computer and potentially grant access to your personal financial accounts to someone who is out to steal your money.

How do you know if a financial management program is safe to install on your computer? If the software came preloaded on your computer when you purchased it, the software is safe to use. If you purchase the software directly from a retailer, the program is likely legitimate and safe. If you download the software from the Internet, use caution. If you cannot be sure the website you download the software from is safe and secure, do not download the software.

Things are not always what they seem on the Internet. A website that looks authentic might actually be a copy of an authentic website and have been put into place by someone who is trying to steal user's personal information. For this reason, always be vigilant about making sure you access the website you intended to use. Do not follow a link to a site sent to you via e-mail or chat by an unknown source or a source you do not trust. If you search for a financial institution's website by means of a search engine, make certain the website you wind up on is legitimate and not a replication created in an attempt to steal your information.

Why should you pay so much attention to safe Internet usage? When your intention is to use the Internet as a means to manage your personal finances, you will undoubtedly input sensitive information such as credit card numbers, bank account numbers, and perhaps even your social security number or mother's maiden name. This type of information is like gold to hackers who want to use your information to access your accounts, steal your money, and open new accounts in your name.

Do not let the threat of hackers and identity thieves stop you from managing your money online, but do be aware that these threats exist. With a little caution and some common sense, you can successfully utilize the Internet to manage your personal finances while also keeping all of your information safe.

CASE STUDY: ENSURING WEBSITE SECURITY

Kyle Robberts, systems engineer, MCP, CEH

Every Web browser is different, but the basics will be the same. If the website you are on starts with "http://," it is an insecure website. If it starts with "https://," then it is a secure website. The difference will be in the level of security though. Most Web browsers will have an icon that looks like a closed padlock. This indicates that it is a secured site. If you see the padlock, the site is secure. The padlock, however does not guarantee that your information is encrypted when it is transferred, which means the data is transformed into a coded series of characters before the information is sent through the Internet.

It is also a good idea to look for the hacker safe emblem on the website itself. This is a relatively new emblem and may not be on all websites. Displaying the emblem on a website means the site was tested for vulnerabilities by an outside resource. This also means the site is much less likely to be hacked into than other sites.

Crafting the Perfect Password

When you load financial management programs onto your computer or register for access to your bank and credit accounts online through the financial institution's website, you will need to create a username and password. Your username does not need to be complicated. In fact, you should make it something that you will remember. Many people use the same username for every website they access. This is a safe method as long as the passwords you choose are effectively crafted. Never make your username and password the same. This is far too easy for hackers or other potential threats to determine.

Each website will have parameters regarding the length of both your username and password. Some sites will have additional rules regarding the characters that can be used in your password. A "character" is a letter, number, or special symbol such as a comma, asterisk, or question mark. For example, some websites will require a certain number of characters that are not letters, such as numbers, the dollar sign, or another special symbol. The use of these special characters adds to your "password strength," which refers to how difficult it would be for someone with limited information about you to guess your password. For example, the last four digits of your social security number or your telephone number do not make for strong passwords, nor do the names of your spouse, children, or pets. If you can take this same information and make it unique by adding special characters or jumbling the information, it will make for a stronger password overall.

Do not write your password down in a place where someone else will find it. If you want to write this information down, do so and keep it in a locked box. This allows you to access the information if needed while keeping it out of someone else's hands. Do not keep a running list of your usernames and passwords on your desk next to your computer. If just one person was able to get a glimpse of the list, he or she would be able to access your account information quite easily.

If at any point you think someone has obtained access to your password, you should change it immediately with every website that uses this particular password. Protect your online passwords as you do your personal identification numbers (PIN) you use for your debit and credit cards. The concept is the same; if someone else gains access to this information, it can be difficult to stop the person from accessing your accounts unless you change the password immediately or close the account altogether.

Make your password something you can remember, but do not make it guessable by other people. This is a very important step when it comes to protecting your information while managing your finances online.

CASE STUDY: CREATING THE BEST PASSWORD

Kyle Robberts, systems engineer, MCP, CEH

Passwords are necessary to make sure you are the only person who has access to your private data. A malicious user or hacker will try to guess your password to gain access to your private financial data. The hacker could then use that information to withdraw funds, open a new account using your information, or conduct other activity that may cause you financial or legal problems.

Because the password needs to be kept safe, it is transmitted by the website in an encrypted format. Because of this, if a hacker intercepts your password, he or she will intercept the encrypted version. The encrypted version usually cannot be decrypted. Because it cannot be decrypted, a hacker will have to try to guess your password and compare the encrypted string of the guessed password to the encrypted string for your password. Hackers do this by running software that uses different methods of trying to guess passwords.

The first method typically used is called a "dictionary attack." This goes through an entire list of dictionary words and compares it to your password. If you use a dictionary word for your password, it will typically be found in less than 30 seconds. If the password is not found in the dictionary, the software will switch to a hybrid attack. This means that the software will go back through the dictionary and try slight variations of each word. If this method fails, the software will switch to a "brute force attack." This means that every possible combination will be used. A brute force attack will in most cases eventually find a password, but can take weeks or months to work.

Keeping this in mind, choose a phrase. For example, suppose you want to use the phase "this is my password" as a potential password. You cannot use spaces, so first you should take the spaces out to make the password "thisismypassword." A combination of capital letters, lower case letters, numbers, and special characters will make a password ex ponentially more difficult to crack. So first, add some capital letters to the password to make it "ThisIsMyPassword." Using character substitution is a great way to add complexity to your password. This can be done by replacing letters with a similar number or special character. In this example, you could replace the "I"s with the number "1," and an "o" with a zero to make the password "Th1s1sMyPassw0rd." Using the same character substitution concept, you could replace an "a" with an "@" symbol to make the password ""Th1s1sMyP@ssw0rd". If you want to add more complexity still, you do not have to replace all of the letters; you can pick and choose which letters to replace. In this example, you could replace one "s" with a $ sign to make the password "Th1$1sMyP@ssw0rd." This would be considered a very solid password and would be very difficult to guess.

LEARN THE LINGO

Logging in: The act of visiting a website and entering username and password information to access secure information.

Software: Refers to programs that are loaded onto your computer, either by the manufacturer or by the user after the computer is purchased. Software can be purchased through a merchant or downloaded directly from an Internet website.

Download: The act of obtaining a program or file for your computer from the Internet. For example, if you want a particular program on your computer, you might be able to visit the manufacturer's website and download the program directly through the site. The program will then be installed on your computer and available for use. Depending on the product, programs can be purchased or downloaded for free.

Hacker: A person well-versed in computers who uses his or her knowledge maliciously to create viruses, gain access to other computers, or take part in other criminal activity.

Certified Ethical Hacker (CEH): This is a computer professional who is employed by companies in order to try to gain access to the company's computer database. The CEH then reports back to the company about the vulnerabilities that allowed the hacker to access the database.

Malicious software: These are programs that are placed on computers without the knowledge of the computer owner. The programs can infect the computer with viruses, spy on the activities of the computer, or turn the computer into a "zombie computer" that sends out e-mails or other activities.

Public Computer Usage

It is usually best to use your own home computer to conduct your financial transactions and review you accounts online, particularly when your home computer utilizes a secure Internet connection and is not used by other people. Sometimes, you do not have a choice regarding which computer you use, either because you travel frequently without a laptop computer or because you do not own a computer at all. If you must use public computers to access your accounts online, such as through a public library or school, extra precautions are necessary.

Computer usage is easily tracked and previously visited websites can be easily discovered. This means you can sit down for a quick session of online bill paying at a pay-per-minute computer — commonly found in cyber cafes and business centers — and the person who uses the computer after you has the ability to access everything you entered, including your username, password, and account number. There are a variety of ways that people can get their hands on your information from a public computer, whether by installing a program that records your keystrokes or as a result of simply forgetting to log off and close the website when you are finished. Also, the person who used the computer before you has the ability to upload software to the computer that can track your information. He or she may plan to come back to the computer later to retrieve the information. Though some places providing public Internet access take precautions to make their computers as safe as possible — such as setting the computer to reboot every time a customer finishes an Internet session and maintaining updated antivirus software — with a public-use computer, it is nearly impossible to stop every potential malicious attempt. You simply cannot be sure that every person who uses the computer does not intend to do you harm. For this reason, you have to be doubly careful when using public computers for online financial management.

So what do you do if you have no choice but to use a public computer to access your accounts online? Use all the tools you have learned so far to make sure you use a secure Internet connection. Upon completion of your Internet session, clear your browser session if the computer does not automatically do it for you. You should also use the same common sense precautions you would use if you were accessing funds through an ATM. Be aware of your surroundings. Make sure no one is looking over your shoulder. Do not step away from the computer while still logged on to all of your personal accounts. There are privacy threats beyond the threats that can be embedded within the computer you use. When you use a public computer — or a laptop computer in public for that matter — to access your account information, make sure no one around you is able to see your keyboard or the information displayed on your computer screen.

CASE STUDY: ENSURING
WEBSITE SECURITY

Kyle Robberts, systems engineer,
MCP, CEH

Public computers are some of the most insecure systems you can ever expect to encounter. You have no control over what the person using that computer before you did on the system. It is very easy for a hacker to sit down at a computer and install software that records every key typed and every click made by any other users who use the computer after the hacker. This means that if you sit at a computer and type your username, password, and bank's website address, it is very possible that all of the information you entered could be sent to a hacker.

If you do use a public computer, be sure the beginning of your bank's website starts with "https" and not "http." This will ensure your information is at least transmitted to your bank in a secured format. Also be sure to click "Log Out" and close your Internet window when you are finished with your session. It is also a good idea to log out of the computer itself when you are done. The best policy though is to not use public computers or public Wi-Fi hot spots to access your personal information. If you do, you have no guarantee of privacy.

Antivirus, Spyware, and Firewall Software

Those who own a computer and are connected to the Internet are at risk of a malicious spyware attack, hacking attempt, spam, phishing scam, virus, worm, and a variety of other techniques aimed at breaking into computers or networks to cause damage, steal or destroy data, or take control over the computer. Any time users are asked to make changes to their browser settings, change their home page, add tool bars, add plug-ins, open e-mail attachments, click on hyperlinks, download software, install software, or respond to questionable looking e-mails, they put their computers at significant risk. One might ask what exactly a person can safely do on the Internet, as most of these activities are performed every day by many users on a variety of websites. This is not meant to scare — most of the previously mentioned actions are safe — and with some planning and defensive tactics, users can prepare to face most challenges and threats on the Internet.

Viruses

Viruses are malicious software designed to destroy or damage data files, operating systems, or the entire computer and are designed to replicate themselves and propagate throughout the Internet by attaching themselves to a file, allowing it to travel to other computers. The most effective viruses spread quickly. The faster a virus spreads and the more malicious the resulting damage, the more successful the virus is. Viruses are primarily spread through e-mail; however, they can be transmitted on disks of every kind — floppy, hard, CD, and DVD — flash drives and reside on hard drives or in other data files. Viruses can be attached to nonmalicious e-mails, meaning the sender of the e-mail likely has no idea that a virus is attached to the e-mail. Viruses can be like time bombs; some are active upon receipt, while others lie in a dormant state for hours, days, weeks, months, or even years before activating and wreaking havoc. Damage from viruses is wide-ranging — from destroying data files, deleting data, deleting critical files in the operating system, reformatting a hard drive, and even replicating through an e-mail program without a user's knowledge. Viruses are executable files — files with a ".exe" extension that are used to install programs — that must be triggered to run, which means that virus files prompt the computer to run a program. Most commonly this is through an attachment to an e-mail that a recipient must open to activate. The virus is often disguised as something else, such as an image or .HTML file. When the recipient opens the file, it activates the virus and it runs, attempting to replicate and execute the damage it was programmed to deliver. The good news is there are plenty of readily available defenses against viruses.

A computer must have updated, active antivirus software running to prevent a virus from infecting it and to detect and remove viruses that have already infected a system. Antivirus software treats a wide array of malware including Trojan horses, computer viruses, adware, spyware, and worms. The amount or type of spyware the antivirus software can treat depends on its version (free and limited, professional and full, or version number, for example) and which company produced it. Most antivirus software products also combat spyware and some have built-in firewalls and other system tools that will meet most or all users' computer security needs. These all-inclusive security suites provide users with one simple solution; however, most are fee-based for both the software and annual update service. Luckily, antivirus software does much more than defend against viruses and identify them when they are found on a system. One of the most powerful features of antivirus software is its ability to remove viruses from a computer. Antivirus software must be configured to scan all incoming and outgoing e-mail attachments. Additionally, users must configure antivirus software to scan their entire systems periodically. It is best to scan the entire system for viruses and spyware at least weekly. Ideally, antivirus software should scan the boot sector of the hard drive, which is the portion of your computer that is responsible for starting programs, upon start up to ensure that viruses have not infected the boot sector of a computer. Again, most of this is included in modern antivirus software.

If you do not already have adequate antivirus software installed on your computer, use a review website to read about the best programs offered. A great source is the TopTenREVIEWS' website (**www.anti-virus-software-review.toptenreviews.com**). Take a look at the reviews of the most popular antivirus software programs, and pay special attention to those programs that offer free downloads online for slightly fewer protection features.

Spyware

Spyware is a combination of the words "spying" and "software" and, like its name suggests, is software that hides in a user's personal computer or network with the intent of collecting personal information, primarily for illicit financial gain. Spyware is defined as anything that resides on a computer and can track, report, and monitor a user's activities (both online and off). Spyware is typically nonintrusive, meaning computer users most likely do not know it is there unless they search for it. Spyware is designed to capture information about Internet users and their activities and report it to someone else. This data might include passwords, financial data, online activity, and keystrokes. Spyware can infect a computer through websites, blogs, software installations, e-mails, viruses, and other delivery methods. Spyware can detect users' keystrokes, steal passwords, copy critical files, steal financial and other data, and intercept e-mails. It can expose all of a user's online accounts for illegal access and cause severe disruption to both home and business finances. Unfortunately, coders — a term for people who write code for programs and websites — create malicious software for fun; for practice; and to test the security of computers, networks, and operating systems to see if they can access private data.

There are ways in which a user can discover whether a personal computer is infested with spyware and there are ways to remove the spyware once detected. A computer user's first defense is antivirus software. Many Internet security suites and modern antivirus software applications have built in anti-spyware protection of varying degrees of effectiveness. There is also software specifically designed to combat spyware. As with antivirus software, anti-spyware software must be updated routinely. Malicious coders have the advantage; they can create spyware and release it into the Internet. After the program is detected, anti-spyware companies must create solutions to detect and remove it. Just like viruses, spyware can be mutated into new versions, which might or might not be detected by anti-spyware software; therefore, regular updating of anti-spyware software will ensure a computer is best protected against infection. Most spyware is spread without the computer user's knowledge, consent, or intent.

Visit TopTenREVIEWS' website (**www.anti-spyware-review.toptenreviews.com**) for a list of the best anti-spyware programs available.

Firewalls

Computer users must have a reputable firewall installed on every computer that connects to the Internet or is part of a network. A firewall is a computer's primary defense against intruders and is a gatekeeper between a computer network or single computer and the Internet. It blocks certain traffic, incoming and outgoing, and monitors all activity to prevent unauthorized access. A firewall allows a person to use the Internet in his or her home, small business, or local area network (LAN) while protecting against hackers, crackers, and other unauthorized users from gaining access to the network and causing damage. Windows® XP (Service Pack 2), Windows Vista, and Windows 7 come with built-in firewalls, but there are many other options available to help protect users' computers and networks from malicious attacks and hackers. A firewall can come in a variety of options: software-based, hardware-based, built into Windows, third-party application, and built into routers. Most software firewalls also include parental controls to manage the type of websites children visit and when and for how long they are allowed to access the Internet. Some Internet security packages also allow users to block inappropriate content and pictures and specific text content they do not want children to view.

Taking into account the threats to Internet security today, many leading vendors have come up with flexible and secure firewalls. There are many choices and it is important for users to do some research in advance to ensure that a firewall is the best for their organization and specific security policies. Not all firewalls are created the same.

Firewalls are typically classified as personal, which is usually used in homes or small businesses, or professional, which is typically used by larger corporations, banks, and government agencies. Hardware firewalls are relatively expensive and used in commercial applications to fight major threats to larger and more complex networks. Some of the more popular hardware based firewall vendors are WebRamp (**www.webramp.net**), SonicWALL® (www.sonicwall.com), Cisco® (**www.cisco.com**), and D-Link® (**www. dlink.com**).

Microsoft Windows firewalls

Windows provides a firewall that is included in the operating system. It was made a part of the operating system in Windows XP Service Pack 2 and Windows 2003 server. The firewall is intended to provide the following features to users:

- Alert the user about incoming connection attempts

- Stop unsolicited network traffic and hide a computer from it

- Monitor applications that are listening for incoming connections and take care of all incoming Internet users

- Prompt the user if any locally installed application makes an attempt to connect to the Internet and also provide the information about the destination where the application wishes to communicate

Systems running Windows XP, Windows Vista, or Windows 7 have a built-in firewall turned on by default. Though the built-in firewalls are not nearly as robust as commercially available firewalls, they provide basic, out-of-the-box firewall protection. Although not the most powerful or customizable firewall software available, these provide robust features and tight integration into the Windows operating system. The interface is simple compared to other firewalls and the features are very easy to understand and manage, unlike some other firewalls. Though these firewalls are adequate for most home and small business users, many will opt for a third-party firewall solution.

Visit TopTenREVIEWS' website to read reviews of some of the most popular firewalls: **www.personal-firewall-software-review.toptenreviews. com.**

CASE STUDY: VIRUSES EXPLAINED

Kyle Robberts, systems engineer, MCP, CEH

A virus is an application of an unwanted program that runs on your computer without your authorization. People write viruses for many different purposes. Some people write them just to see if they can. Some people will write viruses so they can gain access to your computer, and some will write viruses to steal your information. These are not the only reasons people write viruses, but they are the most common. Viruses can cause financial damage to you by sending your personal information to someone who wants to use it for fraudulent reasons.

You can defend yourself against these unwanted viruses by installing an antivirus application. An antivirus application will scan your computer for suspicious activity and compare files on your computer with patterns that match known viruses. This is kind of like comparing a book to a list of known patterns, like how many pages are in the book, how many words are in it, and if it has a certain phrase in it. For example, if the book contains the words "My name is Ishmael," then it would match the Moby Dick pattern. Antivirus programs do this any time a file is accessed or created. It also searches programs running in memory to make sure there is not currently a virus running. However, because some viruses will try to disguise themselves, other methods are used. Some viruses will change themselves. Using the previous example, they may change the line from "My name is Ishmael," to "My name is Bob." This is why antivirus programs also search for virus-like activity. For example, if a program tries to send data in the background without your authorization or load another program without your permission, it will warn you that something is not right.

A virus can get onto your computer in many different ways. If you or anyone who uses your computer uses file sharing applications, such as with work computers or computers that are networked together, they may accidentally download an infected application without knowing it. If you go to a website on accident that is not what you expected, it may try to load spyware or a virus on your computer. Some viruses do not require you to do anything more than be connected to the Internet. The way to protect yourself against a virus is to make sure you have an antivirus application and firewall installed and keep your computer up to date with the most current versions of these programs.

You can make sure your computer is up to date by turning on automatic updates on your antivirus software and in Windows. To turn on automatic updates in Windows, use a search engine to find information on how to use automatic updates with your operating system. For example, if you have Windows XP, search for "Windows XP Automatic Updates." Having a good firewall in place depends on your type of setup. If your computer is connected directly to the Internet, I recommend finding an antivirus program with a firewall as part of its application. If you have multiple computers connected to the Internet from your house, check your router to determine whether it has a firewall installed. Check the manual to find this information.

Computer Maintenance 101

Your computer needs upkeep in order to run its best. Become familiar with the system tools offered by your computer that will help it perform optimally. Although these system tools vary from one operating system to another, you should run the Disk Cleanup utility as well as the Disk Defragmentation utility on a regular basis. The good news is that you can set both of these programs to run automatically at a specific day and time; set them to run at a time when your computer will be on, but you are not likely to be deeply involved in a computer task, as these programs slow your computer's performance.

What are Disk Cleanup and Disk Defragmentation? Disk Cleanup scans your computer's files and looks for files that you no longer need such as temporary Internet files or programs that have not been used in a long time. Reducing the amount of files you have on your computer can speed up the performance. The Disk Defragmentation utility, which is also commonly referred to as a "defrag," moves your files around into a more cohesive grouping. Both of these utilities are important when it comes to keeping your computer running as smoothly and efficiently as possible.

If you are using a PC, find these programs on your computer by looking under the Control Panel. From there, you can run the programs manually or set them to run automatically. Macs do not traditionally need as much recurring maintenance as PCs do, but Mac owners should still familiarize themselves with the methods of maintaining their systems.

Meeting System Requirements

Once you make sure your computer is free from viruses or other malicious software, you need to make sure your computer is able to access all of your account information online as well as any software you download or install. Computer programs have certain system requirements necessary to operate, which means your computer must have enough available space to load and run the program or existing programs needed in order to support the new program. Sometimes system requirements are only suggestions for maximum performance, while others are absolutely necessary in order for the program to run. For example, some antivirus programs cannot be loaded via the Internet and must be loaded using a CD-ROM, so a CD-ROM drive is a system requirement.

Find the system requirements for each program by looking on the box the software came in or, if your intention is to download the program directly from the Internet, read about the system requirements on the website for the program. If your computer does not meet the system requirements, it may not be able to complete the download or it might download the software completely, but the program will not function well or at all. Installing a program that your computer does not have the capability to support can affect the overall performance of your system. You may find your computer performs sluggishly, locks up, or stops working altogether if you load programs onto the system without having the necessary system requirements. If you need to find out how much memory your computer has available, and you own a PC rather than a Mac, you can find this out by looking under "Computer" or "My Computer" on the Start menu.

If you have an old computer, you will probably run into this problem. "Old" is a tricky term when it comes to computers because technology changes at such a rapid pace. For this reason, a computer you purchased a few years ago might not be considered an acceptable system for loading new software. At the very least, you will probably have to update some of the programs already on your computer before your "old" computer will be ready for a new program.

Do you have to run out and buy a new computer in order to manage your finances online? No, although you will want to make sure your computer is as up to date as possible. While you are in the process of scanning your system for viruses, be sure to also check whether there are any software updates available for antivirus program. These updates can be downloaded directly from the Internet.

Keep in mind that if your computer is indeed completely outdated, it may be necessary to look into buying a new (or newer used) computer if you want to get the most out of managing your finances online. An older computer will move slowly and might have more glitches when performing functions. You can take solace in the fact that the prices of computers are nothing like they used to be, so if you originally paid a thousand dollars or more for what was once the top of the line system, you will be pleasantly surprised to find out you can buy a computer that is even faster than the one you currently have for less money. If you do not want to spend much money on a computer, consider a refurbished computer, which is a used system that has been revamped by a technician in order to run well. You can find a refurbished computer in a variety of ways, such as buying directly from a computer technician or from a computer repair shop that additionally sells refurbished computers.

With a newer computer, you might not have to wait as long for programs or websites to load, although this sometimes has more to do with the Internet connection than anything else.

CASE STUDY: UNDERSTANDING CONNECTIONS AND PROTECTIVE MEASURES

Kyle Robberts, systems engineer, MCP, CEH

The requirements to run any software you purchase will be listed on the manufacturer's website or on the box the software was purchased in. Check the requirements against your computer to see whether your computer meets the minimum requirements.

There are two main types of Internet connections. You will have either dial-up or high-speed Internet. If you have a phone line plugged directly into your computer, and you have to initiate a dial-up connection to get on the Internet, you probably have a standard dial-up connection. If your connection is always active, you probably have a high-speed connection. Most high-speed connections will be fine for using finance software.

Antivirus software is used to help protect your computer against malicious software. Malicious software is any type of program written with malicious intent. This includes viruses and spyware. Many viruses can allow a malicious user to connect to your computer and perform various activities. Even relatively harmless viruses can open holes on your computer that will allow other viruses to infect your system. Viruses will also use resources on your computer and make it run slower.

For most people, surfing the Internet can be briefly described as a series of communications between your computer and other systems on the Internet. There are usually multiple conversations going on at the same time, each with a different purpose. A firewall tries to keep unwanted communication from coming into your network or computer. A firewall has a set of rules it uses to decide what type of communication is allowed into, and sometimes out of, your network or computer. Basically, a firewall helps keep the bad things out of your network. There are two main kinds of firewall systems. There is a hardware firewall and a software firewall. A software firewall will decide what communication is allowed into and out of your computer itself. In my opinion, software firewalls are not the best method to use. They are more easily bypassed than hardware firewalls and sometimes cause more problems than they solve. They also may protect your computer, but will not protect other computers on your network. A hardware firewall is a device your Internet connection will physically connect to at one point, and your network will physically connect to at another point. This method will help keep traffic from getting to your computer or network. Most new routers will contain a firewall option. Refer to the owner's manual to find out whether your router has a firewall and how to configure it.

Using an Effective Internet Connection

If you have a dial-up Internet connection, you may not be getting the best connection possible. With a dial-up connection information takes longer to access and files are downloaded and uploaded at a slower speed. How do you know whether you have a dial-up Internet connection? If your computer dials a telephone number in order to connect to the Internet, which may involve hearing a series of noises while the computer makes the dialing attempt, this is an indication that you have dial-up Internet. This also means that your Internet speed is a lot slower than it could be.

In some areas, the only choice people have in accessing the Internet is a dial-up connection. If, on the other hand, the area you live in offers other forms of Internet connections — such as a cable modem or a digital sub-scriber line (DSL), which utilizes telephone lines but usually works much faster than a traditional dial-up Internet connection — you will usually have a much faster and more stable Internet connection. Contact your cable company or other Internet connection provider within your area to find out which services are offered and your options for speeding up your Internet connection. What qualifies as a slow Internet connection? The definition changes as often as technology improves and makes connections even faster. But, you know you have a slow Internet connection if Web pages take several minutes to load or if downloading a program requires hours spent in front of the computer.

Installing a Printer

If you do not already have a printer with a scanner installed on your com-puter, you should obtain one and install it in order to have all the tools you need to manage your personal finances online. You never know when you might need to print or scan a document, so it is a good idea to have this equipment ready to go *before* you actually need it.

The good news is that a decent printer/scanner combo is usually not very expensive. Purchase a printer with both scanning and faxing capabilities. You may also want to explore the option of purchasing a printer with wire-less capability, which will allow you to print documents from any computer in your house — including a laptop — that has the printer software in-stalled. Read the instructions that accompany your printer to find out how to install the printer; you will find that it is not a complicated process.

Backing Up Important Information to an External Source

What would you do if your computer suddenly stopped working? For people who manage their personal finances online using a home computer, this could be a huge problem. You can avoid such headaches by regularly backing up your important files to an external source. Backing up your files involves saving the documents to a source other than your computer, whether it is a flash drive or a back-up service.

You have a few different options when it comes to backing up your computer's information. You can purchase software that will accomplish this task for you, or you can manually back up your files to a CD, external hard drive, or flash drive. There are also websites that will back up all your information to their computers; some of these services charge for this service, and others provide this service for free. No matter which method you choose, the important thing is to actually back up your files so a computer glitch does not throw your personal finances into chaos. For example, Carbonite (**www.carbonite.com**) automatically backs up your computer files and saves them to an external source for an annual fee while Idrive (**www. idrive.com**) offers a similar service for free.

Computer Security Checklist

Use this checklist to make sure your computer is ready to give you the best — and safest — experience when managing your finances online:

- Did you set strong passwords so you are the only person who can access your personal financial information, especially if you use a laptop computer that might get lost?

- Did you scan your computer for viruses, spyware, and any other malicious programs? Did you install a firewall? Did you set these programs to perform security updates and scan for threats automatically?

- Did you perform the necessary computer maintenance to speed up your computer such as disk cleanup and disk defragmentation? Did you set your operating system to receive automatic updates?

- Did you check to make sure your computer meets the system requirements of the financial management software you have downloaded or purchased? Does the software require any other programs to operate at its peak? If so, did you download or purchase these programs as well?

- Is your Internet connection as fast as possible?

- Have you installed a printer on to your computer so you can print financial documents, if necessary?

- Do you have a system in place to back up your computer information to an external source, such as through a website or to a flash drive?

If you are unfamiliar with doing system checks or updates on your computer, it is worth your time to learn more about these simple processes and how they work on your particular computer. The steps for completing these tasks depend largely on what type of computer you have as well as the operating system you use, so if you have not yet taken the introductory tour offered on your computer, you may want to take the time to do so. You can also find help by accessing the website of the manufacturer of your operating system or computer. Some helpful websites include:

- Microsoft (**www.microsoft.com**)
- Macintosh® (**www.apple.com**)
- Dell®(**www.dell.com**)
- Gateway® (**www.gateway.com**)
- Toshiba® (**www.toshibadirect.com**)
- Sony® (**www.sonystyle.com**)
- Apple® (**www.apple.com**)

You will have a much easier experience with managing your finances online if your computer is working at its best. If you are intimidated by the idea of updating your computer, or if you fear there may be something significantly wrong with the way your computer is functioning, you may want to consider hiring an experienced computer professional to look at your system and correct any problems that may exist. Look for a computer technician by searching your local business directory or by contacting the store that originally sold you the computer.

Staying Organized

One of the benefits to managing your finances online is that you will no longer need to keep file folders stuffed with financial statements and other documents. You can keep all this information on your computer and easily access it — as long as you store it correctly.

If you do not have much experience with saving information on your computer, you may be confused as to how you should go about it. This is a relatively simple process, and it is a process that gets easier the more you do it. Depending on which type of operating system your computer uses, the exact details regarding how you should go about creating and saving files to your computer varies. A file is information stored on your computer, labeled by you. Online tutorials are available for any operating system to explain the process in detail; some programs have tutorials built right into them. Look for the "Help" button or a button with a question mark, as these buttons link to information that can walk you through creating new files on your computer or saving information.

Once you do figure out how to create new files for your computer's desktop, create files specifically for saving your financial information. It is up to you whether you want to create one file for all your financial information or if you would rather have one file for each financial institution or

account. Create as many files as you think you need in order to keep all of your financial information situated and accessible. For some people, this will mean one comprehensive file with smaller folders inside of the file, while for other people, it will mean several individual files; do this according to your own preferences.

Create a direct link, also referred to as a shortcut, from your computer's desktop to your financial information, programs, and websites. This will allow for quick and easy access to the tools you use to manage your finances online. As with the creation of individual files, the process of creating an icon for your desktop will vary depending on what type of operating system you use for your computer. If you do not know how to create a shortcut for your desktop, find an online tutorial or use the "Help" function on your computer. It is an easy process and should be quite quick to accomplish. Be sure to label the shortcut so you do not forget where you stored the information.

LEARN THE LINGO

Desktop: The screen you see after logging on to your computer and features shortcuts for various computer programs. Many people additionally personalize their desktops with photos as a background, also called "wallpaper."

Shortcut: An image that represents a file or website. For example, you may have an "e" as an icon to represent Microsoft Internet Explorer. These are also referred to as icons. When you click on a shortcut from your desktop, you are automatically taken to the corresponding file or website.

Operating system: The program your computer uses to present information to you, for example, Windows 7 for PCs or Snow Leopard for Macs. Without your operating system, using a computer would be impossible because there would be no simplified communication between the hardware and the user. You may hear this term abbreviated as your computer's "OS."

Spoof websites: Websites created by spammers that are designed to look exactly like a company's legitimate website, usually for a malicious purpose. For example, a spammer might create a spoof website of a bank in an attempt to collect account information from visitors.

Internet banks: Financial institutions that do not have local branches for customers to visit and are instead available via the Internet.

Website address: The string of letters you use to access a website, usually starting with "http" or "www." For example, the website address for Bank of America is **www.bankofamerica.com**, or simply just www.bankofamerica.com. The technical phrase for a website address is Uniform Resource Locator (URL).

Balance transfer: The process of moving money from one account to another. The term applies both to deposit accounts and credit cards.

Ready to Go!

Once your computer is in order, you are ready to go. Although it may seem like preparing your computer for online financial management is a lengthy process, it is important to take these steps for several reasons. First of all, you need to make sure your computer is not vulnerable to attacks from malicious programs. This is important all of the time, but is particularly important when you intend to use your computer to manage your finances. If an identity thief or hacker gets his or her hands on your personal financial information, it will be far too easy to use that information to steal your money or open accounts in your name. The second reason for making sure your computer is adequate is that you want your computer to run as smoothly as possible. If your computer is not running at its optimum capacity, you will have to wait longer for programs to load or your computer might crash altogether.

A little bit of preparation will make a huge difference. It is far better to prepare your computer now. If your computer crashes, it will be more of a disruption to not have access to your management programs once you rely on your computer to manage your money.

If all of this safety-related information has you boggled or you are thinking perhaps managing your finances online is a bad idea, think again. There are plenty of computer-related books that can go even more in depth and can walk you click-by-click through setting up your programs. Or, if you would rather not deal with the preparatory process or need someone to walk you through everything in person, consider hiring a computer specialist who will come to your home. You can find a reputable company in your phone book or at your local electronics store.

CHAPTER 3

MAKING THE SWITCH TO ONLINE BANKING

Although online banking and online personal finance tools are usually quite user-friendly and are not very complicated, you will have more success if you prepare your computer — and yourself — beforehand.

You should start the process by using the checklist found in Chapter 1 to figure out which accounts you want to access and manage online right away. Remember, you do not have to start managing all aspects of your finances online immediately. Start off slow and at a level you are comfortable with. Which accounts do you most frequently utilize? Which accounts are rarely ever accessed? For example, you may be in a situation where you hardly use your checking account, because you rely on your investment accounts to provide you with a monthly income. Even though for most people the logical first step is to take control of their deposit accounts online, in this instance, it may be a better idea to first conquer your investment accounts and then move on to the other accounts you use less frequently.

CASE STUDY: EFFICIENCY THROUGH ONLINE MANAGEMENT
Teresa, busy career woman

Managing my personal finances online started several years ago when I began tracking my finances through Microsoft® Money. Managing credit card and bank accounts online was a natural progression; you do not have to wait for the monthly statement, and you can access up-to-date information 24/7.

I pay all but one bill online, either through my bank's bill pay system or on the creditor's website. I can control exactly when the payment comes out of my account, and the payments usually posts to my account on the same day that I make them. There is no more worrying if the check will get there on time. Not once have I had a bad experience. Every payday now is a ritual: I check my bank account to make sure the paycheck direct deposit has posted, and then I sit in front of the computer, usually in my jammies, drink coffee, and click "pay bill, pay bill, pay bill."

Making the Move

If you are thinking about switching from traditional financial management to online account management, you may be wondering about the steps you need to take to get started. Most financial institutions make it very easy to make the move to online banking, and the following sections explain the entire process in detail. Making the switch is nowhere near as complicated as you may expect.

Your financial institution

If you have already tried to access your account information online, you have a good idea whether your financial institution offers online access. Even if you have never made the attempt, there is an excellent chance your financial institution has already been urging you to opt in to electronic statements or to conduct your transactions online. Maybe you have received letters from your financial institution outlining all the benefits of online account management or maybe your account statements mention the website address for the financial institution's official website. Although perusing your financial institution's website or meeting with a customer service representative in person is the best way to find out which online banking features are offered by your institution, you should know that there are plenty of reasons why your bank or credit union wants you to start doing your financial business online:

1. **Customers who use electronic banking save the financial institution plenty of money**. The bank or credit union does not have to pay to print or ship paper statements every month and can employ fewer customer service representatives because the customers can process a great deal of their own transactions, such as payments and transfers, online without the aid of a representative. Often, these savings for the financial institution can translate into lower credit interest rates or other perks for customers.

2. **Customers who utilize the resources online can usually find the answer to questions about their accounts or the services offered by the financial institution by perusing the FAQ section of the site**. This means there are fewer customers calling the bank to ask questions or walking into local bank branches to find answers. This

saves the financial institution plenty of time and money because they no longer need to employ as many customer service representatives.

3. **Online access to credit accounts simplifies the payment process**. Customers will be more likely to get their payments in on time if it is easy to do so. For example, a customer whose bill is due in two days may not be able to get the payment to the creditor in time by sending the payment through the mail. When online payments are an option, however, two days prior to the due date is usually ample time to send the payment and have it credited to the account. Keep in mind that not all online payments work this way, so know the terms and conditions of your financial institution's online bill payment system before assuming you can wait until the last minute to make a payment without incurring additional fees.

Managing your accounts online can be advantageous to both you and the financial institution. Additionally, financial institutions know consumers today want to have the option to do their banking online, and this is a top feature customers look for when searching for a new financial institution. It is to the benefit of the creditor, bank, or credit union to make sure online account access and management is not only accessible, but easy to use. They do not want to offer a complicated online account system that will result in a downpour of phone calls from angry customers who cannot use the website to make a payment or transfer money.

It is for this reason you can be sure of a few things: Your financial institution probably offers online access to accounts, the online process is probably quite simple to navigate, and there are probably plenty of ways to get assistance if you cannot figure out an aspect of the system.

How do you know for sure whether your financial institution offers online account access? If you visit a local branch to conduct your financial business, ask a representative about online banking. The representative will tell you everything you need to know about getting online to manage your accounts and may even walk you through the process. Because most financial institutions want their customers to do business online, they have trained staff to eagerly assist in accomplishing this task. If you do not want to go into the local branch to inquire about online account accessibility, call the bank using the same phone number you use when you have a question about your account.

It is up to you whether you want to find the website address yourself or if instead you want to be walked through the process by a representative from your financial institution. Another option for finding the Web address is to look at any paperwork sent to you in the mail by your financial institution. This correspondence often has the official website listed if the institution offers online services. If for some reason you cannot find the website address using any of these methods, consider using a search engine such as Google or Bing to find your financial institution's website. Do this by visiting the search engine (**www.google.com**, **www.bing.com**, or your preferred search engine) and search for your financial institution by name. If all else fails, call a representative at your financial institution to find out how to access the bank's official website.

A word of caution when searching for your financial institution's website using a search engine: Not all websites are what they seem to be. In fact, some Internet-savvy people have the ability to create spoof websites, or websites that mimic official websites for financial institutions and other organizations. You will learn more about spotting a secure versus unsecure website a little later in this chapter, but if you are an Internet novice, you may want to ask someone you trust to help you navigate the initial steps in finding your financial institution's website. You do not need to give the other person your account number or any other personal information, but it can certainly be a big help to have someone who is Internet savvy help you initially. Once you have found your financial institution's site, bookmark it so you will not need to conduct the same search in the future. This will make the process much easier the next time you want to log in and view your account information.

What if your financial institution simply does not offer online account access? Although this is becoming a rarity in today's banking industry, there are likely still a few financial companies that do not offer the option to conduct business online. This can be especially true for smaller institutions or companies only offering short-term products, such as payday loans. The type of financial products they offer may not merit the need for online access, or their small customer base may not justify the added expense of maintaining a website capable of providing these services.

You have two options if your financial institution does not offer online access to account information. You can either accept this inadequacy or find a different financial institution. If you choose to stay with your financial institution, it may be worth it to voice your opinion to the organization to let them know their customers want online account access, but this will probably not result in an immediate push to get customers online. After all, providing this type of service to a broad range of customers does cost money, and even though it is an expense that will usually pay for itself in the end, it is an expense your financial institution may be reluctant to approve nonetheless.

If your financial institution does not offer online account access, it may simply be time to switch financial institutions. This can be a difficult decision to make, especially if you have banked with your institution for quite some time or you like other aspects of the institution, such as their customer service or the interest rates offered for savings or credit products. Here is the good news: There is an excellent chance that you can find these same perks — or ones that are even better — with another financial institution offering full online account access.

Managing your finances allows you to keep close track of your money and may possibly save you money. If your financial institution does not offer online access, this essentially means your financial institution is not offering you everything you need to effectively manage your money. Even if you have been a customer with the bank for several years or you really enjoy certain account features your bank offers, decide how important it is to you to be able to manage your accounts online. The same goes for credit card companies, lenders, prepaid debit card providers, and any other institution that provides you with a financial service. It is your money; you have the right to access the account at any time. A financial institution not offering online access is simply not a fully functioning financial institution in today's market.

Signing up

The actual process of signing up for online banking varies from one institution to another, but the general process involves creating a username and password. The financial institution will verify that your account is valid by comparing the information you provide with the information the financial institution already has on your account. You might also be asked to verify your request, which is usually done by verifying receipt of an e-mail sent by your financial institution. You might also be asked to provide additional information, such as your ATM or check card number, your PIN, the last four digits of your social security number, e-mail address, or the language in which you would like to view the website. You might also be required to read and acknowledge an electronic communications disclosure. Again, the process of signing up for online banking varies from one financial institution to another. If you have questions regarding the process that is required by your bank, contact a customer service representative from your financial institution.

Make the switch

Suppose you check with your financial institution and it does not offer online account access, the access that is offered through your financial institution is limited or, worse yet, there is a monetary charge for online banking, and you have decided to switch financial institutions so you can access your account information online. What should your first step be?

Use the Internet to help you find the best financial institution available. Although you can certainly benefit from speaking to your friends or family members about the banks or credit unions they use, the Internet offers a wide variety of tools to help you compare several institutions at once. You are not only looking for a financial institution with free online account access and other helpful online features; you are also looking for a financial institution with great customer service, attractive interest rates, and all the account features you want, such as:

- Instant account access around the clock
- Low interest rates for credit products
- High interest rates for savings products

You do not have to give up the other things you want in a financial institution — such as helpful customer service representatives and that "small bank" feel — in order to access your account over the Internet. Today, there are many financial institutions with the total package: online account access, great account terms, and efficient, friendly customer service.

Whether you are switching your deposit or credit accounts, use the Internet to find out which companies are rated highly for all the features you are looking for. Here is a brief list of some of the best websites that allow you to compare the various offerings available:

- Bankrate (**www.bankrate.com**)
- CreditCards.com (**www.creditcards.com**)
- FindABetterBank (**www.findabetterbank.com**)

Visit these websites to find out which financial institution has the features you are looking for. These sites will tell you which financial institutions offer the highest savings account interest rates, the lowest credit interest rates, and free online account access.

Internet-only banks versus traditional banks

Some banks operate only online and do not have branches for customers to visit. If you are not familiar with conducting financial transactions online, this may seem like a risky idea. If you are concerned that an Internet-only bank might be a bad idea, know this is a healthy concern. You should never assume that everything online is what it appears to be. That being said, many Internet-only banks are safe, secure, and offer exceptional interest rates and financial products. It can cost less to operate an Internet-only bank than it does to operate a bank with local branches, so Internet-only banks can pass these savings along to their customers in the form of better interest rates and fewer fees.

There are some potential drawbacks to Internet-only banks. In order to withdraw money from your account, you will need to use an ATM sponsored by another bank. Online-only banks do not have ATMs located around the country, and using another financial institution's ATM will result in extra fees added to the transaction by the host bank. ATM fees can be reduced by looking for banks that do not charge fees — although very few banks do this — or shopping around to find out which banks offer the lowest fees. You can also plan ahead and receive cash back while shopping at your grocery store or other merchant offering this option. Most grocery stores do not charge fees for cash back when using a debit card to make purchases, so this is definitely a viable way around the fees charged at ATMs. Another drawback to banking with an Internet-only institution is that all deposits, other than direct deposits such as a paycheck, must be made through the mail. If you make cash deposits frequently, this could become cumbersome and a security risk for the funds being sent through the mail.

It is not necessary to turn to an Internet-only bank in order to get the best online account access. Most major financial institutions — and plenty of the smaller ones as well — have fantastic online account access and management while also offering the opportunity to visit a local branch if necessary. Use the websites listed above to compare financial institutions to find out which bank or credit union is best for your needs.

If you do switch to another financial institution to gain online account access, whether for your deposit accounts, credit accounts, or both, do not close your account at one financial institution until your account is opened at the new financial institution. You should also make sure any existing automatic payments or recurring direct deposits are transferred over to your new account before the old account is closed. You certainly do not want to close an account in an effort to simplify your finances and then wind up actually complicating things quite a bit. If you have automatic deposits or withdraws on the account and close the account before switching these to your new account, checks or withdrawals will be rejected and deposits will be returned to the sender, which might result in extensive fees.

Ask a representative at your new financial institution if they offer switch kits, which simplify the process of switching financial institutions. This allows you to sign one form to have the balances from your previous accounts sent to your new accounts. Not all financial institutions offer switch kits, but do take advantage of the kit if it is offered to you.

If your switch is to a new creditor, do not stop making payments to your previous creditor until after you know remaining debt balances have been moved to the new creditor. Even if the new creditor initiates a balance transfer on your behalf, you are responsible for the payments to the previous creditor until the balance transfer is complete.

"My husband and I use USAA online banking for absolutely everything. I could not live without it. I have automatic payments going out, and I also input random bills into the system with the account number and address and pay through my USAA checking account. USAA sends the check out for me. I love online banking and wouldn't have it any other way."

— Patti, mother of two

LEARN THE LINGO

Internet-only banks: Financial institutions that offer services solely through the Internet and do not have local branches for customers to walk into. These financial institutions may have telephone numbers to call for assistance, but the primary means of communications is through e-mail and online chat.

Before you make the switch to a new financial institution for the purpose of gaining access to your accounts online, make sure the financial institution has the type of online access you are looking for. Just because a financial institution advertises that customers have the ability to access their accounts online does not necessarily mean the financial institution offers the capability free of charge or online access to each of your accounts.

There are certain things your online banking experience should include. There are certain features that should absolutely be a part of the online banking system, and there are some features that not all financial institutions offer, but are certainly attractive perks. How many of these features does your financial institution provide?

Online Banking Feature Must-Haves

Speak to a representative or visit your financial institution's website to find out which online banking features are available. The following is a checklist of features that should be offered through your financial institution if they offer online access to your checking or savings accounts:

- **You should have constant access to your account transaction information**. With the exception of times when the website is down as required for system maintenance, you should have the ability to access your account information any time. Online banking is supposed to be convenient. If you can only access your account information during limited times of the day, the convenience factor is negligible. Additionally, the transaction information you view for your account should be current and as up to date as possible. Though it is not possible for all information to be completely correct all of the time, such as with preauthorized or pending transactions where the actual purchase amount has not yet been posted to your account, when possible, you should have full access to what is happening with your account.

- **You should have transaction details that are easy to understand**. This means you should be able to view the date or a transaction, the amount, and where the transaction took place. Instead of a vague transaction descriptions such as "Purchase: $25," the transaction listing should tell you where the purchase was made. Trying to figure out your spending trends will be incredibly difficult if you cannot determine where your purchases are being made.

- **You should have free access to your accounts online**. Most financial institutions offer online account access free of charge, so there is no excuse for paying for this feature. If anything, your financial institution should be grateful you choose to do your banking online because this can potentially save them quite a bit of money. Charging customers a fee to utilize online banking does not make sense, and you should not expect to be charged for this service. Additional services, such as online bill payment, may feature nominal fees, but simply viewing your accounts online should not come with a cost. In fact, because online bill payment has become a standard feature, most financial institutions no longer charge a fee for this type of service either.

- **Your financial institution should offer secure Internet banking**. This is incredibly important because so much sensitive personal information is transmitted via online banking. There is an extremely good chance that the online banking offered through your financial institution is safe and secure, but you should be able to view exactly what type of security features your bank features. Look for a privacy policy at the bottom of your bank's main Web page. If anything, your financial institution should boast about the many security features they have available. This information should not be difficult to find, but if you have a hard time tracking this information down, you should wonder why your financial institution is not eager to share this information. After all, there are some security measures that are more effective than others; your financial institution should take all necessary precautions — and then some — to ensure your financial information is safe online. *You will learn more about making sure the websites you visit are safe in the next section of this chapter.*

- **The online banking experience should not be incredibly complicated**. There is no reason for your financial institution to offer a complicated online banking service that the average user cannot figure out how to use. Though it is reasonable to expect that Internet novices may need a little more tutoring and practice before they feel comfortable with using online banking services with confidence, the average user should be able to figure the system out with little effort. It should be a simple process to access the accounts, view transactions, and transfer money from one account to another. If the financial institution makes this a difficult process, it is reasonable to assume that many of the institution's customers may stop using the service altogether.

The function of an online banking system is to offer an easier way for customers to get account information and conduct routine banking transactions without the need to enlist the aid of a representative. The essential features of online banking should be offered free of charge and should not be so complicated that people stop using the service to access their accounts.

If the online banking features offered by your financial institution do not provide you with basic services free of charge, it may be time to look for a different financial institution.

Online financial management can mean many different things to different people, but most people think about online bank account management when this topic arises. In particular, most people think of managing checking and savings accounts online.

Most people who do their banking online have aspects of the process they really love while also having aspects they wish they had the ability to change. The good news is that there are so many different online banking programs available that you are bound to find one that works well for you. Whether you do your online banking solely with your financial institution's website or you utilize other programs available online to manage your finances (such as Mint.com [**www.mint.com**] and Wesabe [**www.wesabe. com**]), you will find there are some features that are completely helpful and others for which you do not care. No financial management program is perfect; although, there are some with features that may be of more use to certain people.

Begin the process of managing your money online by accessing the online banking website offered by your financial institution through your Internet browser. If an online tutorial is offered through the website, you should be sure to utilize this feature. Tutorials are designed with a wide variety of Internet users in mind, so even if you rarely spend time online, you will probably still be able to follow the instructions provided in the tutorial. The tutorial may also show you features available you may not have found on your own. If you have questions about using the online banking function after you have completed the tutorial, find out if there is an educational database that answers FAQs for online banking users. Look for any of this information by browsing the website's list of topics or by using the search engine within the financial institution's website.

Not all financial institutions offer virtual tours through the Internet banking system; although, this is becoming common as more customers turn to Internet banking. It is far easier — and usually more cost effective — for financial institutions to create and offer a tutorial than to provide live staff to guide customers through the use of their online banking function over the phone or in person. At the very least, most financial intuitions that offer online banking have an FAQ section in an attempt to answer questions before customers feel compelled to call a bank representative or walk into a local branch to ask about aspects of the online banking program they do not understand.

CASE STUDY: ONLINE BANKING IS GREAT, BUT NOT PERFECT

Trudy, busy professional

I use and prefer online banking; although, I wish the options offered through the online services were a little more interactive, as in they allowed me the ability to input checks or upcoming withdrawals that match up as they come through my bank account.

I have been lucky thus far to not to have any major issues with online banking, but the online bill pay service I use is not very good at projecting the time frame that the payment will arrive to the recipient. My payments have arrived late from that account a few times, and this is really frustrating.

It would be great if there was a "place holder" of sorts where you could enter your handwritten checks and when the check for that amount comes through, it registers it with your prior entry. But I will also say that I love the ability to pay bills and manage my finances online; although, at the same time, the possibilities of someone accessing my personal information do concern me.

- **Spending tracking**: One of the most interesting — and potentially beneficial — features offered by some online banking services is the ability to track and correlate debit card spending. This feature takes information from the purchases you make using your debit card and presents you with a report that analyzes your spending. Information regarding your spending habits might be presented as a listing or a graph and will give you a good idea of how you frequently spend your money and may point out some areas where you can save. For example, if the report reveals to you that 30 percent of your income has been going to eating meals at restaurants, this should be a wake-up call that you might want to start cooking at home. This feature is becoming more common with online credit management, but is a feature occasionally appearing on banking websites for debit card expenditures.

- **Easy depositing**: You may never have to walk into your financial institution's local branch to make a check deposit ever again. Many online banking services have started offering interesting and innovative ways for customers to make deposits without having to mail in a check, go to an ATM, or walk into a branch. Now that financial institutions have the capability to electronically collect on written checks based on the account and routing number, your financial institution may never need to physically obtain a check from you to credit your account. Many banks and credit unions have started offering customer the option of electronically depositing checks by scanning the check and e-mailing an image of the check to the financial institution. Some institutions will even accept an image of a check that has been obtained using a camera phone. If you receive checks on a regular basis, yet do not want to have to physically present the check for deposit to your financial institution, look for an online banking service that allows easy options for depositing checks.

Some financial institutions offer special "Internet accounts" that are designed specifically for people who intend to utilize the Internet for the majority of their banking needs. These accounts usually feature many of the perks listed above at no extra charge, but collect additional fees to conduct financial business outside of the realm of the Internet. If your financial institution offers an account like this, and you plan to switch the majority of your account management to the Internet, ask about changing the account type as long as there are no fees involved in the switch.

A few words about online usage fees: Avoid them. Online banking is becoming far too prevalent for financial institutions to justify charging customers to access their account information online. Unless you are getting extra special features from your bank, do not accept additional fees as an unpleasant fact. Though managing your finances can potentially save you money if you utilize all of the available services to your advantage, paying additional fees for these online services does not make much sense.

Electronic Communication

Signing up for electronic statements is an important step you can take right now, regardless of whether you stay with your current financial institution or decide to switch to a new institution.

Electronic statements, also called e-statements, are sent directly to your computer via e-mail instead of through the mail. Many financial institutions also provide downloadable statements that can bee accessed simply by logging into your online banking account. For banks that allow customers to download statements online, an e-mail is typically sent to inform customers that a new statement is available. In most instances, e-statements contain all the information a traditional statement contains such as account transaction dates and amounts and any fees assessed. The benefits to electronic statements are numerous:

- You may receive your e-statement faster than you would receive a paper statement, because it does not have to work its way through the U.S. Postal Service.

- Some e-statements are interactive, allowing you to create graphs or charts that analyze your spending and saving habits.

- You can easily save copies of your e-statements on your computer, alleviating the need to find space in a filing cabinet to store your financial files.

- If you do decide you need a paper copy of your e-statements, you can print the statement using your home printer.

- E-statements eliminate the risk of someone stealing your statement out of your mailbox and using your account information to steal your money.

- Because no paper is used to create your account statement, the e-statement is better for the environment and is the "green" choice. You will find many financial institutions urging account holders to make the environmentally friendly choice and switch to e-statements, but remember that this method of statement delivery also saves the financial institution plenty of money. These savings may potentially be passed along to account holders in the form of fewer fees.

Sign up for electronic statements by visiting the financial institution's website or by contacting a representative. Signing up is usually as simple as clicking on an e-statement acceptance link on the financial institution's website or instructing a representative to enroll you in the e-statement program over the phone or in person. Keep in mind that if you try e-statements and find that they are not a good fit for you, you do have the ability to stop receiving e-statements and continue receiving the statements through the mail. Speak to a representative to find out whether your financial institution provides this option and how to remove yourself from the e-statement program if you decide to do so.

If for some reason you are not comfortable with the idea of receiving electronic statements, try requesting e-statements while still receiving paper statements through the regular mail. Most financial institutions will give you the option of receiving your statements using both methods because they know most people will eventually switch to only receiving e-statements after realizing the ease and convenience.

You may also want to look into additional options offered by some financial institutions. At the request of the customer, some banks and credit unions will no longer send a statement at all — through the mail or e-mail — and will instead allow customers to simply access their statements online as needed.

Online Banking Security Features

Many financial institutions offer additional features in order to ensure your security when you attempt to access your account online. Some may ask for an additional password or PIN, others may display an image unique to your account profile (often called a sitekey), and some offer a special word to verify you are on the authentic website. For example, Armed Forces

Bank (**www.afbank.com**) assigns an image to each online account as well as a verification word. A customer of this financial institution might be assigned an image of a tiger and the verification word "Apple." Every time this customer logs on to access his or her account online, the customer should see the image of the tiger and see the word "Apple" before reaching the account access area of the website. This tells the customer that the website actually belongs to Armed Forces Bank financial institution and is not a spoof website created by someone attempting to steal account information.

It is important to note that most financial institutions also require account holders to set up security questions that require you to verify your identity. For example, if you attempt to access your account information from a computer you have never used, the website will not "recognize" the computer and a predetermined security questions might need to be answered before access is granted to your account in order to ensure your identity. You will have already answered these questions when you initially set up your online account, and the questions must be answered correctly when prompted by the website in order to gain access to your account. Common questions include, "What was the name of your high school?" or "What was the name of your first pet?" If you do not remember the answers and respond incorrectly too many times (as determined by the financial institution), you might be locked out of your account until you can verify your identity by speaking to a customer service representative. You might then be given the opportunity to change the answers to your security questions.

Changing your password varies from one financial institution to another. You might be required to submit the change of password request to the bank in writing with a signature, which will then be compared to the signature the financial institution has on file for you. In many instances, this will then mark your account as approved for a password change, and you will then change the password in person or online. Other banks might require you to answer a series of personal questions such as your mother's maiden name and your social security name before your password can be changed. If your PIN must be changed, your financial institution may require you to accomplish this using an automated telephone system.

The following are a few unique security features that are offered by some financial institutions:

- Free enrollment into credit monitoring services.

- Credit and debit cards with photographs of the authorized user on the face of the card.

- Check security safeguards, such as water marks and anti-copy features.

CASE STUDY: RELYING ON THE INTERNET

Anna, college student

If the Internet ever fails, I would have a hard time managing my finances. I have never managed my finances on paper because the Internet has always been available.

I really like that there is no paper involved with online banking. It is easier to get online than it is to wait for the mail. I really like the convenience.

I have not run into any problems with e-statements. I save money on stamps because I pay all of my bills online. Every month I log in to my account and pay my bills myself. I do not have them set to be paid automatically because I am afraid that if everything is automatic, I might get lazy and things will not be paid.

I also pay my college tuition online, and I use the Internet to view my balance and special fees. I even order my books online using my university bookstore's website and plan to use the Internet to do some comparison shopping for my textbooks to save a little money.

Account Management and Monitoring

The ability to manage and monitor you accounts online may be the single biggest perk of Internet banking. If an error occurs on your account or if a deposit you are expecting does not get credited to your account in a timely manner, you will be able to monitor the situation closely and react more quickly than if you were waiting for a paper statement to come in the mail. With online account access, you can view the same information regarding your account that a customer service representative can view. You may be able to view pending transactions, including pending direct deposits, which will help you plan how your money will be spent.

How often should you view your account information? You should always check your account when you are waiting for a pending deposit to clear before you make the assumption the amount has been credited to your account. Far too many people assume that a deposit has cleared and begin spending that money when the money is not yet available, which usually results in hefty overdraft fees. Too many incidents of negative balances may actually result in the account being closed by the financial institution, whether the customer wants the account closed or not.

Even if your payments to creditors, utility companies, and other bill collectors are set to automatically be deducted from your checking account, it is a good idea to check your account periodically to make sure these bills have been paid. After all, no computer system is infallible. When using automatic payments, do not assume that the payments has been made. Though you should not feel obligated to check your account each day, it is a good idea to review your account on a regular basis to make sure your bills have been paid on time.

Online banking should take some of the effort out of money management, but it does not make it a completely automated task. You are still responsible for knowing how much money is in your account and making sure your bills are paid. Telling a creditor that your bill was not paid because your online bill pay service functioned improperly is not usually reason for most creditors to refund late fees or not raise interest rates. You can avoid this situation by reviewing your online accounts to ensure everything was debited and credited as scheduled. It does not have to be an intense process, but it is a necessary one nonetheless if you want to retain control over your finances.

After you have gained more experience with online banking, the process will become much easier. You will get a feel for how transactions are reported and how long it takes for automatic payments to be made, and it will take less time to review your account on a regular basis.

LEARN THE LINGO

Routing number: The nine-digit number that uniquely identifies your financial institution. You can find this number on the bottom left side of your paper checks or by checking your financial institution's website. Make sure you have the proper routing number for your financial institution before giving to it someone else to make a deposit into your account because an incorrect routing number will send the funds to another financial institution.

Direct deposit: An automatic deposit of funds into your checking or savings account. This method of depositing is common for payroll or other recurring deposits. You must grant permission for someone to set up a recurring direct deposit into your account.

Wire transfer: A type of electronic transfer of funds from one account to another.

Direct electronic debit: A withdrawal from an account that occurs electronically.

Checkbook reconciliation

One of the most important tasks necessary for effective money management is the reconciliation of your checking account statement each month. This is also referred to as "balancing a checkbook" and essentially involves making sure the information you have recorded regarding the transactions and balances on your account corresponds with the information the financial institution has reported on the statement. By reconciling the statement each month, you can make sure there are no errors — either your own or on the part of your financial institution — and you can also make sure no one has accessed your account and used it without your permission.

You will need to make the decision whether maintaining a checkbook register while managing your finances online is necessary. Some people still prefer to maintain a paper checkbook register, at least in the beginning, until they understand that they can rely on the Internet banking to keep record of their account transactions.

If you are already well versed in managing your personal finances, you probably already spend time each month reconciling your bank statement. The good news is that online tools can make this process much faster, more accurate, and in some cases, nearly completely automated. Some online programs will keep your account transactions up to date by recording your transactions, including deposits and withdrawals, so all you have to do is to make sure the balance listed by your financial institution matches the information you have listed within your other online money management tools. When you consider how much time and effort this will save you, it is easy to see the benefit to transferring this process online instead of using a pencil, paper, and a calculator. Of course, you can always choose to do both in tandem, but you will soon realize there is no need for it as long as you monitor your accounts online.

You have a few different options when balancing your checkbook using on-line tools. There are many different programs to assist you with reconciling your bank statement. Check your financial institution's online banking services to find out whether it offers the option to export all of your account transactions to financial management software. You will need to have the program already loaded onto your computer before taking advantage of this option, but once the program is ready, it is a very easy process to send all of your information to the money management software. The process usually only involves clicking an "export" button and waiting while your account information is sent to the program. Information regarding your account transactions are then exported to your financial management software and are available for your review. If your financial management software also provides recommendations regarding spending or other financial matters, the program will then be able to provide those recommendations based on the information imported.

If you do not want to utilize the export feature, you can still use the online account information provided by your financial institution to help you reconcile your bank statement. Compare the information in your own records with the account information on your online banking account to ensure that both balances correspond. In fact, with online banking, you do not have to wait until the end of the monthly banking cycle to make sure your own records correspond with what is reported on your account. You can reconcile your own records any time you want as long as you have access to your account online.

Many financial institutions offer virtual checkbook registers online, so if you still want to maintain a checkbook register, yet want the ease of using the Internet to track your account activity, find out whether your financial institution offers a similar feature.

Most online banking sites allow you to print a list of transactions that were made during a specific range of dates. This means you do not need to print a complete statement if you do not need this information; simply specify the dates you require and print the necessary information or view it online without printing at all. Concerning unauthorized transactions on your account, keep in mind that an online chat, e-mail communication, or telephone conversation with a financial institution representative might not be sufficient to preserve certain rights granted to you through federal laws and enforced by the Federal Trade Commission regarding how to dispute errors on your accounts, whether it is an error on the financial institution's behalf or an instance of theft. If the institution needs more than ten business days to research the problem, the error should be removed while it is being researched. For this to happen, you must initiate the dispute correctly. In most instances, you will be required to submit notification in writing detailing the fraudulent activity on your account. Doing so using the Return Receipt service through the U.S. Postal Service will only further your ability to prove you alerted your financial institution of the fraudulent activity should you need to prove your actions sometime in the future. When it comes to getting fraudulent transactions removed from your account, remember the most important steps you can take: recognition, reporting, and documentation.

TEXT AND MOBILE BANKING

Do you want to receive text alerts on your mobile phone when your account balance is getting low? Your financial institution might offer this feature along with other texting and mobile banking features including the ability to text a request for your account balance or recent transactions. Although the steps to sign up for text banking vary from one financial institution to another, it usually involves visiting the financial institution's mobile website, entering your mobile telephone number, and then verifying a security code that is sent to your phone.

With mobile banking, many financial institutions allow customers to find nearby branch locations, access account and balance information, make transfers, and even pay bills — all from their cell phones. Mobile bank websites offer encryption technology to protect your account from unauthorized access.

Online Account Transfers

When your money is in an account you can access electronically, you have the ability to transfer money from one personal account to another from your computer. This can be a useful tool when you want to move money from your checking to your savings account or vice versa, and you have the option to transfer money on a one-time basis or to set up recurring transfers that will occur at the same time each month until you cancel the transfer order. You can also transfer money to other people's accounts within your financial institution or accounts held at other financial institu-

tions. The process of getting money from one account to another has b simplified immensely by electronic banking.

One-time transfers

Suppose you are preparing for a vacation and you want to have access t some extra spending money while you are away. You would prefer to sim ply use your debit card to make purchases instead of repeatedly pulling money out of an ATM because of the potential fees you might incur for using ATMs outside of your financial institution's network. You have extra money in your savings account and you want to move that money from your savings account into your checking account for use on your vacation.

Before Internet account access became commonplace, you had a few options. You could walk into your local branch and fill out a transfer request. Some financial institutions allowed customers to call a representative over the telephone to request transfers between accounts. Some banks also allowed customers to transfer money between accounts using an ATM; although, fees might be charged to the customer depending on the ATM and institution.

Fast forward to modern day and the convenience of online banking: Making a transfer from one account to another can be as simple as logging on to your account, telling the system which account to transfer a certain amount from and what account to send it to, and clicking the "transfer" button. With most financial institutions, there is no wait for the transfer to take place, even if the online transfer is done outside of business hours. For example, online banking customers of Wells Fargo can complete transfers by logging into their accounts, clicking a link to go to the transactions page, selecting the account from which the money will be send and the account to receive the money, and submitting the information.

When transferring money from one account to another, it used to take a day for the funds to be deposited into the account. Now, the money is instantaneously credited to your account. This can be incredibly convenient if you have to make a transfer right away that you were not anticipating. Suppose you are on vacation and need more money than you originally budgeted for. As long as you have Internet access — even if it is through the Web browser provided on your cell phone — you can transfer money from one account to another to give you instant access to the cash you need. This is a stark contrast to the effort it used to take to conduct a one-time account transfer. A process that used to involve paperwork and a signature can now be accomplished while riding in the back of a taxi with a cell phone. In some cases, these account transfers can also occur between deposit and credit accounts, especially if the accounts are all held at the same financial institution, with the same ease. Most banks charge fees for this service, so make sure to check with you bank first.

CASE STUDY: USING A CELL PHONE TO ACCESS YOUR ACCOUNT
Will, college student

I switched to online banking because I am pretty busy all the time; I work about 85 hours a week. I do not have a lot of time to sit down with a check register, so I do it all online. I would estimate that by using online tools, I save at least an hour a week, especially because I track all my receipts. With my work schedule, saving time is really important. I use Microsoft Excel spreadsheets to track my spending an keep me on a budget. I do not have the spreadsheet correlated to a program yet, but I am planning on looking into it to save even more t

The only problem I have ever had with paying my bills online is that I did not realize there would be a delay for the bill to actually be paid. The online bill payment system I use requires a day or two before the payment is delivered to the person I am paying, depending on which creditor I am paying. Once I realized this, it was fine.

I do not think I could use my old method of paper tracking anymore to manage my money. I use my cell phone to access my Wells Fargo account online approximately 75 percent of the time when it is time to pay my bills. They offer a really great online bill pay service, and I like that I can do it on my phone. At first I was worried about the security of conducting financial business on my phone, but really, my phone is the closest thing to me. I always know where my phone is — usually before I know where my wallet is. I worry more about losing my wallet than I do my phone, so to me, this is safe.

I do not know if you could say that I have saved money by managing my money online, but I have really saved a lot of time. They say time is money, so I guess in that regard, I have saved money by doing my finances online.

Recurring transfers

There are many reasons why you might need to transfer funds from one deposit account to another on a recurring basis. Many financial experts urge people to set up an automatic transfer from a checking account into savings account so the act of saving for the unexpected becomes an automatic act. Many people have several deposit accounts they use for various reasons, such as a family account and another individual account. Still other people open deposit accounts jointly with parents or children in an attempt to contribute financially and decide to automatically transfer regular amounts to the account on a recurring basis so the financially dependent person will know how much and when to expect the money.

Online banking can be used to not only initiate these recurring transfers, but to also manage the transfers once they are in place. You should check to make sure the transfers are occurring as scheduled and for the amount requested. Changes to the transfers can also be made online including changing the amount of money that is transferred and the date the transfer takes place. This is usually a very simple process. Most online accounts have a Web page for existing transfers where users can view the transaction history and pending transaction schedule. Changing the amount or date of an automatic transfer — or cancelling the recurring transfer altogether — commonly involves clicking on a link that states wording such as "Adjust Transfer Information."

Other types of online transfers

Sometimes, you might want to transfer money to an account held by someone else. While you always have the option of mailing the person a check, you might prefer to do this electronically. Depending on the capabilities of your financial institution, you might be able to transfer money electronically from your deposit account into another person's account. Often, the process includes logging on to your account, clicking on "transfers," and then specifying the transfer to another account at the same financial institution. You might need to manually input the account number unless it is an account for which you are also an authorized account holder, such as an account for your child. Not all financial institutions offer this feature online. *There are also options for transferring funds using online methods beyond those available through your financial institution, such as using PayPal®, which you will learn more about in Chapter 8.*

If you want to transfer money to an account at another financial institution that is not in your name, a wire transfer might be one of many solutions. A wire transfer is an electronic transfer of funds from your deposit account to another deposit account at another financial institution that is either in your name or someone else's. This is a helpful feature if you need to quickly send money to a friend or relative or transfer money from your account at one institution to your account at another institution. These transfers do not occur instantaneously and the length of time it takes depends not only on your own financial institution, but on the receiving financial institution as well. In fact, most methods you use to transfer money from your account to an account at another financial institution under someone else's name are going to take a varying amount of time before the deposit is accessible to the receiver. Also, there is usually a fee associated with wire transfers, which varies from one financial institution to another. There are also monetary limitations associated with this type of funds transfer as set by the Federal Reserve, but if you want to send a relatively small amount of money, you will probably not encounter any limiting restrictions.

Although you may have the capability to conduct a wire transfer online using your financial institution's website, you may be required to verify your request with a signature. This is for security reasons and to verify someone else is not requesting money to be sent from your account to theirs without your consent. Once your signature has been received and verified, however, your financial institution may allow you to request further wire transfers to the same account online. In addition to your signature, you will need the routing number and account number for the receiving account. Make sure this information is correct before requesting the wire transfer because if your financial institution tries to transfer the funds without the correct information, it may take a few days before the mistake is realized and another couple of days before you get the money back. If any of these days fall within a weekend, it can take even longer.

Although not all financial institutions have the capability, find out about a direct electronic debit (also known as an electronic check) if you want to transfer money from an account at one institution directly to your account at another institution. If both accounts are in your name, even though they are at separate intuitions, you may be able to request a direct debit from one account through the receiving institution. For example, with Pentagon Federal Credit Union (**www.penfed.org**), customers simply need to access their account online, click on "transfers," specify a direct electronic debit, enter their account information, and click submit. The funds are immediately credited to the receiving account. If your financial institution offers this type of transfer, they usually also offer the opportunity for customers to request the transfer online. There are two distinct advantages to this type of online account transfer. The amount is often immediately credited to your account, and the fee for this type of transfer is usually significantly less than other forms of transfers involving another financial institution, perhaps because it is between two accounts with the same account holder and does not involve customer service representatives. In fact, some financial institutions conduct this type of transfer free of charge. There are usually daily transfer limits for this type of transaction, but if you need to simply transfer a few hundred dollars from one account to another, this can be one of the best options if it is offered by your financial institution. Check your online banking account for a link relating to money transfers. If you do not see this type of link online through your online banking account, contact a representative to find out if this type of transfer is possible.

If the person you are sending money to needs the money as quickly as possible, consider a Western Union funds transfer. Request this service through your financial institution if it is offered or request the funds transfer using the official Western Union website (**www.westernunion.com**). This type of funds transfer usually costs more than a wire transfer for a few reasons, including the fact that customers are willing to pay the fees and merchants are usually the fund distributors, but there are some advantages to this method depending on your situation. Western Union allows you to debit money directly from your account and electronically send the funds to a Western Union location. The recipient of the money transfer goes into that location, which might not be a financial institution and could be a drug store or other merchant, and shows identification in order to collect the money. This can be a fast way to send money to someone who needs some emergency cash, even if that person is located in another country. There are many foreign Western Union locations. In fact, Western Union boasts a huge array of overseas locations, so it is simple to send funds electronically to someone vacationing overseas or to friends or relatives who live in another country. Keep in mind that the person you send money to should be prepared to present photo identification. In some cases, he or she will need two forms of photo identification. You might also be asked to set a password the recipient must know in order to collect the funds from the Western Union location.

Western Union can also be used to electronically send money to a debt collector, which is called Quick Collect. With this method, the money you owe gets to your creditor or collection agent more quickly than it would if you utilized other methods. This method is usually used when a bill is delinquent and is not a method you should use routinely to pay your recurring bills due to the high fees associated with the money transfer.

Online Deposits

Technology has made it incredibly easy to make deposits online compared to traditional means of making bank deposits. Not too long ago, deposits were always made by walking into a local branch and presenting a check for deposit to your account. Eventually direct deposit became the norm for payroll and other recurring payments, which made the process much easier but could not accommodate sporadic checks or money orders that needed to be deposited into an account.

Most institutions offer customers the opportunity to mail checks into the bank for deposit, which alleviates the need to make a trip to the bank or credit union. There are a couple of potential problems with this process, however. There is always the chance that a check mailed for a deposit can wind up lost in the mail or stolen. Additionally, there can be a significant delay between the time the deposit is sent by the customer to the time the funds are actually credited to the account. This is not such a huge hassle if the check is a small amount and the customer is not relying on the funds to pay bills, but if the check is for a significant amount and the customer needs the money as soon as possible, the potential delay can be a real problem.

Depositing through an ATM can cut down the processing time involved with getting the money credited to your account, but it still requires a trip to the ATM. Also, if an error occurs with the ATM and the deposit is attempted during non-business hours, the customer will have to wait until the financial institution reopens before the problem can be fixed. If the error occurs on a Friday evening, and the financial institution does not open again until Monday morning, this can be quite a long time to wait for the deposit to be credited to the account.

For these reasons, financial institutions have begun offering some very innovative ways to make deposits online with no need to walk into the local branch or visit an ATM. In fact, many financial institutions now offer the option to deposit checks without ever physically surrendering the check at all.

Scanning deposits

You may never have to walk into the branch of your financial institution again to physically deposit a check. Many banks and credit unions now offer the option for account holders to simply provide the financial institution with an image of the check, either by using a computer scanner or by snapping a photo of the check using a mobile phone equipped with a camera. One of the first financial institutions to offer this feature was USAA (**www.usaa.com**), but many financial institutions do not offer this feature yet at all.

How can financial institutions do this? The fact is that all the information a financial institution really needs to process a check for deposit is the account number, the routing number, and the amount of the check. The account number and routing number are both featured along the bottom of the check; the routing number is a nine-digit number that tells your financial institution which bank or credit union the money comes from, and the account number tells your financial institution specifically where to draw the money from. Every financial institution has a unique routing number, and every account within a financial institution is assigned an account number.

Scanning a check is simple, especially if you are already well versed in the process of scanning an image. Scan the check just like you would scan a photo or document. If you have never used your scanner before, you may want to check the instruction manual to find out how to properly work the scanning function.

The process of sending the image to your financial institution will vary depending on its specific requirements for scanned deposits. If your financial institution merely requires that the image of the check be e-mailed to a specific e-mail address, you probably have a couple of options for sending the image via this method. While some scanners offer you the option of e-mailing the image directly from the software associated with the scanner, this process can become complicated if you do not know the default e-mail address your computer will use. It can also be difficult to ensure that the e-mail went through.

Another option is to e-mail the image using the e-mail account you use to send other e-mails. You can simply save the image onto your computer's hard drive and attach the image in the e-mail you will send to the bank. The specific steps involved in this process vary according to your computer and the e-mail account that you use, but the general steps for most e-mail accounts are quite simple. Select the option to compose a new e-mail and input the recipient's e-mail address, subject line, and any accompanying text in the body of the e-mail message. Click on the "Add Attachment" button — the wording may be different depending on your e-mail provider — and attach the image of the check. Do this by finding the image wherever you have saved it on your computer. It may take a moment before the attachment has been added to the e-mail, but you will know your attempt was successful when the image is listed as an attachment. The faster your computer, the faster this process will be, but the entire process usually takes less than a minute.

Some financial institutions do not want the image of the check sent through e-mail but instead provide a website where you can upload the scanned image for deposit. If this is the case with your bank or credit union, you will have to follow the instructions provided to you to load the image onto the website. The process is usually just as easy — if not more so — as sending the image via e-mail and may involve similar steps, such as uploading the attachment onto the website. It is a good idea to go through any online tutorial offered by the financial institution regarding scanned deposits before you try to submit a deposit this way to be sure you perform the process correctly and the deposit is credited to your account as soon as possible. How long will the deposit take before it is credited to your account? Procedures vary from one financial institution to another, but in many cases a portion of the deposit — or the full amount, in some instances — is credited to your account immediately.

Online banks and credit unions are not the only institutions that offer the option of scanning checks for deposits. Many financial institutions with local branches offer this option as well. If you are not sure whether your financial institution offers this method for depositing checks, check its official website or speak to a customer service representative.

In some instances, utilizing a scanner to electronically submit a check for deposit is not necessary. Some financial institutions, including USAA, allow customers to capture an image of the check using a mobile phone and submit the image via the mobile Web. As this technology becomes more popular it will become more prevalent, but not all financial institutions currently offer this deposit option. Furthermore, not all mobile phones are equipped with the necessary technology. Ask a representative from your bank or credit union, or log on to your bank or credit union's website, to find out whether this deposit option is available and if your mobile phone is eligible to use for depositing checks. Signing up for this service will involve registering your mobile phone with the bank and installing the mobile banking application on your phone. This process will vary from one financial institution to another. Through the application, you can take a picture of the check and submit it electronically over your phone to the financial institution.

Many people are initially apprehensive about the scanned deposit option because this is a completely different way of making deposits than they are used to. On the other hand, many who try the process are delighted by the ease of use and plan to continue utilizing the method in the future.

Ordering Replacements

What do you do if you are running low on paper checks? What if you want to order an additional credit card for a family member? Most financial institutions now make it incredibly easy to order replacements online with just a few clicks of the mouse.

Credit and debit cards

If you want to order a replacement debit or credit card, keep in mind that there are different procedures involved if the original card was lost or stolen. It is one thing if you need a new card because the magnetic strip on the back of the card has worn down and stopped working or if you absolutely know for sure that you card is somewhere in your car but you just cannot find it; it is an entirely different matter if you have no idea where your card is or you are fairly sure that someone has stolen it from your wallet. If you think that your card has been lost or stolen, you may not be able to deal with this situation completely online because some financial institutions require that you speak to a customer service representative to cancel the card's functionality and order a new one. Check with your financial institution to find out what the procedures are if you encounter this scenario, but remember that the main objective in this situation is to act quickly to stop someone else from using your card.

Find out if your financial institution offers the option to order credit or debit cards online by checking the financial institution's website or speaking to a customer service representative. You will likely be able to order additional credit or debit cards online if you simply want to add an authorized user to the account. Log in to your online account and look for a link relating to ordering replacement cards or look for a customer service link. The directions will lead you through a process that should not be fairly quick and easy. You will receive the card you ordered within a few weeks; although, some financial institutions will allow you to request that the card be sent to you more quickly, which usually entails additional fees. Although some financial institutions allow customers to request a new card via the Internet, some require customers to make this request either over the telephone or in person at a local branch.

Keep in mind that ordering the card via the Internet rather than visiting your local branch and speaking to a representative does not mean exempt you from fees associated with ordering the card. A replacement debit card fee is a common fee charged by financial institutions. If your bank or credit union usually charges $10 for a replacement card, you can expect to have that amount deducted from your account even when you send the request electronically.

Checks

Even though paying bills online has made check writing an infrequent occurrence for many people, it is still a good idea to have checks on hand in case you need them. You have two options when ordering checks online: You can order directly through your bank or credit union, or you can use a check printing company.

Most financial institutions make it very simple to request new checks, especially if you do not want to change the color or theme of your checks. As long as you last ordered checks directly through the financial institution, everything will automatically be pre-filled, including the check numbers. If you want to change the font, theme, or any other aspect of the checks you order, you will be able to make these changes using the online system. After logging in to your online bank account, look for the link relating to ordering replacement checks or customer service.

Not all financial institutions allow you complete the entire ordering process directly within their website. You may be directed to a check printing company the bank or credit union uses, but in many cases, all of your information will be imported over, so this will still minimize the effort it takes to order checks.

The other option you have for ordering replacement checks online is by using a check printing company, such as Checks Unlimited® (**www.check-sunlimited.com**) or Deluxe™ (**www.deluxe.com/products-services/personal-checks.jsp**). You will have to input all of your information and be sure to include correct information regarding your checking account, but often, this option is less expensive than ordering directly through your financial institution — unless, of course, it offers checks free of charge. Be sure that the check printing company is legitimate and the order is accepted on a secure website, as you will need to provide your account information and may also have to provide a debit or credit card number to pay for the checks.

Other online self-service options

You financial institution might offer other self-service options beyond ordering checks. You might be able to request a stop payment on a check, order copies of your statements, change your address, and obtain a balance transfer for your credit card. The convenient online services can save you from needing to visit a local branch to make these requests.

Need Help?

A website feature that is becoming quite popular among financial institutions is online chat or instant message (IM). This allows customers to log on to their accounts and enter into a one-on-one chat room with a customer service representative. Whether your question is about opening a savings account with your bank or receiving clarification about a charge that showed up on your transaction log, it can be more convenient to have a quick IM conversation with a representative rather than making a phone call or walking into a local branch.

Find out whether your financial institution offers this feature by checking its website or asking a customer service representative. If your financial institution offers this option, it is usually a matter of clicking a button that says "Click Here to Chat with a Representative Live" or something that is similarly worded. This will either lead you to a new website or open another window on your screen. Depending on how busy the chat representatives are, you may have to wait a few minutes before you get to ask your question, but in the interim, you may have the option to continue accessing your account information until the representative becomes available. When the representative is ready, the chat will begin with the representative welcoming you to the chat function and asking you what assistance you need, to which you reply with your question. This is the common procedure for most financial institutions offering an online chat feature with customer service representatives.

Chatting online with a customer service representative can have benefits as well as drawbacks. If you do not like the format of online chat, which involves typing your question and awaiting a typed response, you may be frustrated by this method. On the other hand, if you just need to have a quick question answered and do not want to wade your way through the automated calls usually associated with contacting a financial institution by phone, the chat function is a good option. Another potential drawback is that you may have to wait a while for a representative to join the chat, and if your computer runs slowly, the process may be drawn out even longer, because it will take your computer longer to send and receive responses. Another benefit, however, is that you can keep a printed transcript of the conversation you have with the representative, which can be quite helpful if you need to prove to your financial institution that certain things were said by the representative later.

CASE STUDY: BANKING OUTSIDE OF STATE

Elizabeth, busy mother

My husband does all our banking online because our bank is located in Anchorage, Alaska and we live in Omaha, Nebraska. This enables us to keep a bank we really like even though we no longer live near the bank. He also pays our bills online, but we do not use the bank for this service because it charges $5 per month for online bill pay. We pay bills with each individual creditor at their websites.

Sometimes direct deposits show as a pending transaction, but then debits are made that take us into the negative, so we have to be careful to make sure the deposit has been credited before we try to utilize the funds.

We are glad we can stay with the bank we like even though we no longer live close by. The bank we have offers shared banking with some of the banks here in town, so we can make deposits at local banks without fees. We use online banking for transfers but not for deposits.

CHAPTER 4

ONLINE BILL PAYING

You may be one of the many people who have never delved into the realm of online bill paying, which includes paying bills through a bill pay service offered by your bank or a third-party service or via the creditor's website. There are several reasons why people do not try this option. Some people tell themselves that they have never had problems paying their bills before so why switch? Others might be apprehensive about providing account information via a website because they fear their personal information will wind up in the wrong hands. Still others might not know how to get started, so they never bother trying. Whatever the reason, once they try it, plenty of people quickly realize that paying bills online is simple and quick.

You have a wide variety of options when it comes to paying your bills online. If your main goal is to simplify the bill paying process, you can use a bill payment service — such as PayTrust, ChoicePay, or a service provided directly through your financial institution — that pays all of your monthly recurring bills for you directly out of your checking account. If you are uncomfortable with the idea of an automated service handling your bills, or if the amount of money you owe every month varies, you can pay your bills using the website of the creditor to which you owe money. You can mix and match your online bill paying methods to match your needs and comfort level. Most of the methods you choose will either be completely free or will only require a small fee. Online bill pay is now considered a standard feature rather than a perk by most financial institutions and is a common feature of creditors.

Get Started

Before you can begin paying your bills online, you need to find out if your creditors accept payments electronically; although, you will likely find that most creditors offer this service. Keep in mind that some bill payment services will write checks on your behalf and send them via postal mail to your creditors for you, so you may still be able to use an online bill payment service even if your creditor will not accept payments electronically.

If you want to use a third-party online bill payment service, you might be able to input the names of your creditors for your recurring bills into the website or software and have the bill payment service tell you if each creditor accepts payments electronically. You also have the option of contacting your creditor directly and asking about this option. If your plan is to pay your bills individually through the creditor's website, finding out if electronic payments are accepted is as easy as visiting the official website for each creditor. Most creditors —whether for loans, credit cards, or even utilities — allow, and encourage, online bill payment. It costs the company much less to accept electronic payments than it does to accept payments through the mail, which must be processed by an employee. For this reason, most creditors are eager to accept electronic payments and make it easy for customers to take advantage of this service.

There are many different online bill payment services to choose from, and for this reason, it is important for you to take a look at the options and learn how to properly use the program you choose. Do not assume that an online bill payment service — either through a financial institution or another source — will offer a particular feature or perform a certain task. Instead, find out for yourself what the bill payment service's capabilities and features are.

Online payments with a creditor

Making payments online using a creditor's website is usually a very simple process; although, initially, you will have to register with the website as well as provide information regarding the bank account you want the payment withdrawn from, such as your account and routing number. Registering is usually very simple, especially if you have your account numbers right in front of you.

Once you have a valid online account with your creditor, look for a link that takes you to your current statement or account information. This will show you your account activity and how much money is due with the next payment and when that payment is due. When you are ready to make a payment — or to set up a scheduled recurring payment — look for the link for payments and provide your deposit account information (if this information is not already in the system), the amount of your payment, and what date you want the payment made.

When making payments online, you may have the option of paying with a credit card or having the payment withdrawn electronically from your checking account. Whichever option you choose, you will need to provide information to the company so it can process the payment. If you want to pay with your credit or debit card, you will need to provide the credit card number, expiration date, the full name listed on the front of the card, and in some instances, the security code, also referred to as the card verification value (CVV) code, located on the back of the card. If you are paying with your checking account, you will have to provide the account number and the routing number, which you can find on the bottom of your checks, preprinted deposit slips, or by contacting your financial institution.

Companies you want to pay online — whether the bill is a recurring debt such as loan payment, a utility payment, or a one-time payment for a service — may require some additional steps if you want the payment withdrawn directly from your checking account. You might have to go through an authentication process, which usually involves the creditor depositing a small amount of money into the account and requiring you to log back on to their website to verify the amount of the deposit. The amount deposited is usually less than a dollar and might come in two deposits, but the entire process usually does not take more than a couple of business days to complete. This step may seem annoying because it initially slows down the process of making your first payment, but this is designed for your own protection; the process is intended to make sure that you actually have access to the account from which payments will be made. An example of a creditor using this method is Chase.

You can set up one-time payments — a payment that only occurs once — or recurring payments — a payment that happens every month until you cancel it — through most websites. You will also probably be given options regarding the type of recurring payment you want to make, including the date that you want the payment made and the amount of the payment. When you request that a payment be made through a website, do not forget that you made the payment. In other words, do not set up a recurring payment for your credit card every month on the due date but then forget that this amount of money will automatically be deducted electronically from your checking account.

Pay close attention to the information provided to you when you make a one-time payment via a creditor's website such as a confirmation or receipt code. Though some creditors will immediately credit your account with the amount of the payment, others will delay crediting the amount for a day or two, so plan accordingly. Also, it is important to note that most creditors offer online bill pay free of charge, but many charge a fee to customers who need to make a same-day payment. These fees can be costly, so avoid waiting until the last moment to make payments online. You may find that some companies charge a convenience fee for simply making payments online, but this practice is dwindling and becoming less common.

Online payments with a bill pay service or your financial institution

Your financial institution might offer bill payment services online as an additional option or as a feature of your checking account. To find out whether this option is available through your checking account, read the terms of the account, contact the a bank representative by phone or visit in person, or research the topic on the financial institution's website. Whether your financial institution offers this service free of charge, for a monthly fee, or on a per-transaction basis depends on the bank or credit union you use. If your financial institution does not offer online bill payment services, you have two options: You can either switch financial institutions, or you can use an online bill payment service separate from your financial institution. There are plenty of these services available online, some of which are free and others that charge for this service on a monthly or per transaction charge.

The features offered by an online bill payment service, whether directly through your financial institution or a separate source, usually include attractive features in addition to the ability to pay bills electronically. Some services accept and catalog electronic statements from your creditors so all of the information is available to you in a logical format simply by logging on; other services issue paper checks to creditors at you request as long as the recipient has a mailing address. There are also services that allow users to upload information for more than one checking account, which allows for multiple payment options. With so many options, it is worth it to take a look at more than one service to find one that works best for you. An Internet search for bill payment services will yield many results, some suitable and some illegitimate. You can also find out whether your financial institution endorses certain companies.

You should expect to pay for an online bill payment service that is separate from your bank or credit union, but often, the amount you pay will be less than what you would have paid in mailing costs associated with sending payments through the U.S. Postal Service. Be sure the service you choose is legitimate by reading reviews online and checking with the Better Business Bureau (**www.bbb.org**). You will be providing the company with a wide variety of personal information, including account numbers for both your credit accounts and checking accounts; this is not information you want to land in the wrong hands.

Start your search with some of the more popular online bill payment services such as Quicken Bill Pay (**http://quicken.intuit.com**) or Paytrust® (**www.paytrust.com**). Although the setup for the online bill payment service will vary from one program to another, the process usually involves following prompts on the screen. Most services are very user friendly and will walk you through the entire process, but the processes vary from one service to another. You will spend some time entering account numbers and setting dates for the payments to be made, but once everything is in place, you will find that the process is quite simple. In fact, with most services, payments can be made automatically each month as long as your payment amounts do not change. If payment amounts change, you will have to adjust this information in the system, which is not usually a difficult task. Be prepared to pay a monthly fee for these services, which is typically around ten dollars.

For most people, it is the simplification of the process and the consolidation of information that makes online bill payments appealing. For example, using Quicken Bill Pay will allow you to export all of your payment information to your Quicken software program loaded on to your computer, which you can then use to balance your checkbook. If you are used to manually paying bills and recording all this information into a checkbook register, you may be pleasantly surprised at how simplified the entire process can be when you use the online tools available to you.

When shopping for an online bill payment service, keep in mind that debt consolidation services such as Consumer Credit Counseling Service are not an online bill payment service for consumers who are up to date on their bills and do not need assistance with debt renegotiation. Do not sign up for one of these programs under the impression that it is a traditional online bill payment service.

One-time payments

The Internet is a great tool to use when making one-time payments, even if you choose not to utilize a bill payment service. For example, if you want to pay for your newspaper subscription and the option of paying online is available, log on to the newspaper's website and make your payment. You may have to register with the website in order to use this function, so be sure you have any information regarding your account and payment method handy to speed up the process.

The money for the payment is deducted directly from your checking account or credit card account, and you will not need to bother with stamps and envelopes or worry about the threat of lost checks in the mail. Do look out for additional fees that some websites charge for this option, which are sometimes referred to as convenience fees. Using the above example, if the newspaper website charges customers $3 to process each online payment, it makes more sense to sent the payment through the U.S. Postal Service in this instance — unless you do not mind paying a fee for the convenience of paying online.

Account transfers

If you owe money to another individual and are repaying the person either in installments or in one lump sum, you may be able to transfer the money directly from your deposit account into the account of the person you owe money to.

This is especially easy if your account and the account of the other person are with the same financial institution. Set up an automatic transfer through your financial institution's website by looking for a link that refers to transferring money. You will need the other person's account information in order to do this. Input the other account number and set up the recurring payment for whatever amount and day you want the money transferred. You can then monitor the payment each month if you set up a recurring payment. Lists of your transactions and transfers in your online account can also serve as a record of your timely payments in case you should need proof in the future.

Some financial institutions charge a fee for this type of transaction, but most will allow you the option to complete the payment like you would any other account transfer. Peruse your financial institution's website to find out more information on setting up an account-to-account transfer.

CASE STUDY: UTILIZING
ONLINE TOOLS

Gabe, military veteran

I do not really use Mint.com (an online money management website) to the fullest extent that I could, but it definitely has some very interesting tools on it. At Mint.com, you can set up an account that, should you give it permission, will monitor all of your financial interaction. It is quite amazing. The service pulls information from your bank and any other accounts that you give the program access to, such as E*TRADE Financial or another bank, and it monitors how much you have in each account and how you have spent your money. The service shows trends and even gives you a pie chart showing where you have spent your money. It also offers a budgeting tool that you can use to develop your personal budget. Mint.com can also offer money savings advice based on your spending habits and trends.

I have a Mint.com application on my iPod that allows me the same access that I have on the website as long as my iPod® is in Wi-Fi range.

CHAPTER 5

ONLINE MONEY MANAGEMENT

Managing your finances online is much more than reviewing your account information and paying your bills over the Internet; although, these things alone can simplify your finances quite a bit. There is also an array of money management tools available on the Internet, many of them free, that you might want to try. After all, if you do not manage your money effectively, there may not be enough money in your account(s) to pay your bills online. You can use the tools available to you on the Web to keep your finances under control and help your savings grow.

Online budgeting tools can help you learn more about composing a budget, tracking your spending, and saving to help grow your budget. Use an online spending log to figure out where you are spending your money and how you may be able to save some money by curtailing your spending. You can also use online tools to determine your actual net worth and help you decide what you should be doing with your financial assets, such as whether you should add more to retirement or increase the amount of money that you put toward investments. Calculators offered on Bankrate. com can help determine your net worth.

If you have never spent time perusing money management tools available online, you may be amazed by the range of products and services on the Web. Not only can you find informational websites to help you understand what you should be doing with your money, but you can also find interactive tools to assist you with making financial decisions. Some tools will ask a series of questions regarding your debt and income and then, based on your responses, provide recommendations. This can be especially useful if you are the type of person who does not really care for crunching numbers and analyzing data to make the best decision regarding your money. Information that once could be found only in financial books or directly through a financial adviser is now readily available from a variety of online sources.

Online Budget Tools

A budget is a written plan detailing how your money should be spent. To build a budget, you should subtract the amount of money you spend on various expenses, including recurring debt payments, utility payments, and other things such as groceries and gas for your car from the income you have coming in from employment or other means. A budget can show you where you may be spending too much money and help you see where you may be able to cut back your spending in order to pay down debt or put more money into a savings account. If you already compose a budget, you probably know that this is one of the single most important money management tools you can use. You may also know that writing and maintaining a budget can be relatively time-consuming, and for this reason, some people stop using a budget. Extensive effort is required to compose, modify, and maintain a written budget, especially when you are doing all of this with paper, pencil, and a calculator.

The good news is that there are plenty of online budget tools available that will not only help you compose your household budget, but will also maintain the budget for you and show spending habits that may point to an area within your budget where you may be able to cut back on your spending in order to save more money. These tools offer more than a budget that is written out on a piece of paper; the online services turn the budget into an interactive tool that can assist you in analyzing where your money is currently spent compared to where your money should be spent. Some of these online services will provide pie charts that categorize how you are currently spending your money and might make suggestions for improvement. For example, if the pie chart reveals that you are spending just as much money on Starbucks as you are on your monthly car insurance premium, the program will alert you to this and may make the suggestion that you scale back on your coffee habit. Some online budget tools are merged with your checking account, which allows the program to update your spending information without any additional effort on your part.

Using an online budget tool can simplify your budgeting exponentially. Managing your money is much easier when you do not have to spend a great deal of time analyzing and revising how you plan to spend and how you actually spend your money.

Choosing an online budget tool

Financial software, such as Quicken and other popular programs, usually features an option for creating and maintaining a budget. If you decide to buy software or have done so already, it would make sense to use this option. However, if you have not already purchased the software, you do not have to go out and buy such programs because there are many free budgeting options online.

If you are looking for an online tool that will simply assist you in creating a budget, many options are available. Many websites offer free templates that can be downloaded directly to your computer that can assist you in composing a budget. These templates are already prefilled with common expense categories and spaces for you to input your income and expenses. Choose a secure website offering these templates and download the document to your computer by following the prompts. After the template has been downloaded to your computer, you can access the document by clicking on a shortcut you create on your desktop or by retrieving the file from your hard drive and modify it as necessary, adding your own budget items and deleting any information you do not need. Save the template to your computer each time you make a change to the budget, and reference it often to ensure you are keeping your spending in check. You can find websites offering these free downloads by conducting an Internet search, or you can go directly to a website that offers free forms — such as the official Microsoft Office website (http://office.microsoft.com) — and search through the available household budget templates that are offered free of charge. Before you download any budget form, read the system requirements. For example, one of the household budget spreadsheets offered through the Microsoft Office website requires Microsoft Excel to function properly. Other sites offering these forms will have varying system requirements, so read the information offered on the website thoroughly prior to starting the download.

LEARN THE LINGO

Excel: A Microsoft program designed for mathematical and graph functions. This program can be used to create budgets and track spending.

iPhone: A smart phone that provides Internet access and applications. Many iPhone users access financial account information using these phones.

Budget: A plan for how your income should be spent. For example, a budget might specify that 10 percent of your income will go into a savings account or that $320 is paid for your auto loan every month.

Net worth: An amount that specifies your financial worth after all your financial liabilities are taken into consideration. For example: If you have $10,000 in the bank, yet owe $2,000 to a creditor, your net worth is $8,000.

Net worth calculator: An online tool that estimates your net worth based on the information you provide, such as the amount of money you have in deposit accounts and your total debt.

Financial adviser: A person who acts in a professional capacity to provide financial advice to individuals for a fee.

If you are looking for an online budget tool that is more interactive, you have plenty of options available, many of which do not cost any money to use. Some of the more popular online budget tools will merge several of your accounts, such as multiple deposit and debt accounts, and track where your money is being spent. For many people, looking at all of their accounts together in one place helps them to figure out what their next financial step should be. They will also make suggestions regarding ways you can better manage your money. Review the following websites to find one that appeals to you and offers the budget tools you need:

- **Mint.com (www.mint.com):** Of all the free online budget tools, Mint.com offers one of the most comprehensive programs. Not only will this website assist you in composing a household budget, but it will also track your transactions with any of the deposit and/ or credit accounts to which you grant Mint.com access. This might not be an option for you if you are uncomfortable with giving account information to a free budgeting website, but because Mint assures visitors that the information is secure and safe, many people do indeed trust this website with their information. In return, users receive assistance with composing a budget and monitoring all account transactions, and they also receive detailed reports that point out areas within the user's budget that should be revised to optimize savings. This website can be accessed through the Internet on a computer or with an iPhone® or other phone with Internet access.

- **BudgetSimple (www.budgetsimple.com):** This website will allow you to create a budget for free. It will also create spreadsheets and graphs that allow you to visualize where your money is being spent. BudgetSimple does not feature all of the bells and whistles of Mint. com such as personalized financial recommendations, but it is a great website for people who simply want to compose a budget and track their spending.

- **moneyStrands (www.money.strands.com):** This free online service tracks your spending and provides recommendations based on the data imported from your financial accounts. The advantage to this website is that your information is available from any smart phone. Another unique aspect to this website is that the free program is married to a social networking platform, so not only can you manage your money, but you can also chat with other users about how they manage their money.

- **Budget Stretcher (www.homemoneyhelp.com)**: This free website offers a wide variety of forms pertaining to personal financial management including budget spreadsheets and bill summary ledgers. This website also offers resources to assist users with saving money such as links to coupon websites and other frugal living advice.

- **BudgetTracker (www.budgettracker.com)**: This website tracks spending by importing your account information from your financial institution and makes suggestions to create a budget. This website will even allow you to create shopping lists and send "I Owe You" notices to people who you owe money to.

- **Financial institution websites**: Do not forget to consider the websites of the financial institutions with which you already do business. Many of these banks, credit unions, and creditors offer free budgeting tools on their websites and may allow you to import and export data from your account into the budget. This is a good option for people who do not want to provide account information to other budget websites. The downside is that some of these sites do not allow you to import information for accounts from other financial institutions, so you will have to manually enter this information yourself.

There are also plenty of websites available that charge a monthly or one-time fee for access to their online budget software. Unless there you do not want to use one of the free websites previously listed for a particular reason, it is recommended that you start with a free budget website. There are so many free budgeting websites that paying for one does not make a lot of sense unless you are looking for a unique feature not offered by a free website.

The following is a list of some of the websites that charge a fee for accessing their money management programs:

- **OrganizeMyMoney.com** (**www.organizemymoney.com**): The products offered through this website include a one-on-one consultation with a financial adviser. This can be a good option for people who feel overwhelmed with organizing their finances, because the financial adviser assigned by the website will help customers get started. The cost of the consultation is approximately $300 and is a one-time fee for the services.

- **Dave Ramsey's MyTotalMoneyMakeover.com** (**www.mytotalmoneymakeover.com**): This is the official website for Dave Ramsey, a popular financial expert who champions for debt-free living. Some money management information is available for free on this website, but if you want to attend a class, get full access to the money management tools, or speak to a financial adviser, you will have to pay a fee. The cost of the financial management classes and financial advice varies.

- **Quicken** (**http://quicken.intuit.com**): This is an example of a website offered by a company that manufactures personal financial software. Though some of the information on the website is free, you will must obtain the software or pay extra fees to utilize all of the available personal financial management tools. In some instances, additional fees exist even if you purchase the software, such as the monthly fee to utilize online bill pay. This software varies in price depending on which version you choose and where you purchase it, but you can expect to pay anywhere from $30 to $100.

Crafting and managing a household budget online may be one of the single most important things you can do to get your personal finances into order. Once you have a handle on how much money you have, how many bills you have, and how you are spending your money, you will be poised to take control of your finances and start managing them effectively. If you find that you struggle with your finances and feel as though you have no idea where your money is spent each month, there is a good chance that utilizing online budgeting tools can turn your finances around. The fact may be that you have an adequate amount of income, but you just have not been utilizing it correctly. An online budgeting tool can reveal this to you and help you determine how you should handle your money.

Online Spending Logs

If you decide to use Mint.com or BudgetSimple for online budgeting, you will also have the option of utilizing the spending logs available through these websites. Spending logs track what you spend, where you spend it, and what category each purchase falls into by creating a spreadsheet or graph containing this information. For example, if you use Mint.com, a debit card purchase at a restaurant will show up on your online spending log in the category of "Food" or "Dining Out." The importance of a spending log is obvious; when you know how your money is actually being spent, you can decide if you are making the right decisions with your money. Unlike a budget, which tells you what you should do with your money, a spending log is a reflection of what you actually do with your money. There can be a big difference between the two.

Mint.com and BudgetSimple — and similar websites — will present the information to you in graph form. If you would rather view this information on a spreadsheet, or if you are just looking for a website that provides you with a spending log spreadsheet you can maintain on your own, there are many such sites available. You may have the capability of creating a spending log on your own with programs that are already loaded onto your computer, such as Excel or even Word®; however, when you utilize some of the tools available on the Internet, it can make the upkeep of a spending log — and the analysis of how you spend your money — easier to manage.

Spending Diary (**www.spendingdiary.com**) and BudgetTracker (**http:// budgettracker.com**) are two examples of websites that offer free spending logs. To simplify your finances, however, it is a good idea to use one website that not only assists you with your budget, but also gives you the capability to create and maintain a spending log such as Mint.com. Merging all this information into one website will give you a better picture of your spending and saving habits.

Most websites that offer spending logs are free to use. Some may ask for you to register with the website and agree to receive newsletters or other forms of advertisements from the website and affiliates. A website that offers a free service should not ask you for your credit card number. Do not give your credit card number to a website that you do not intend to purchase something from.

The method you use for managing the online spending log will vary according to which service you utilize. With some sites, you manually log each purchase under the proper category and then use the log as a whole to analyze your spending. On other websites, all of the information for the spending log is imported from your deposit and credit accounts, and then the data is analyzed for you and presented in a variety of forms. Most of the spending logs offered online are quite simple to navigate and many offer demos and tutorials that will guide you through the entire process and explain everything in simple terms. Look for a link on the site similar to "Take a Tour," "Online Demo," or "Help" to learn how to use the program.

If you have tried to maintain a paper spending log in the past and found it to be a time-consuming or annoying task, you will probably find that doing so online is an entirely different experience. It is not nearly as lengthy a process and is much simpler than writing down every single purchase, adding up all your purchases, and manually deducing how you can decrease your spending and maximize your savings. Do not allow a previous tedious attempt at logging your spending to dissuade you from using an online spending log to help manage your finances.

If you choose an online spending log that automatically imports your spending transactions from your credit and debit card usage, you will likely only need to review the reports that are produced by the program. If, on the other hand, you choose a manual online spending log, you will have to dedicate a little more effort to the process because you will need to compose the spending log manually instead of an automated version. Whichever method you choose, know that you are taking important steps to manage your personal finances more effectively by using the tools provided to you on the Internet.

CASE STUDY: MANAGING YOUR MONEY ONLINE

Andrea Travillian, MBA, financial life coach, owner of Smart Step, Inc.

I provide money and life tips for free and offer free teleclasses for people to take. As with any other online financial professional, when someone wants more detailed information beyond what I have already provided for free, the customer should be prepared to pay for the service. If customers are not paying for the services they are receiving, they should ask themselves, "How is this person making money, and can I trust the answers they are giving based on how they are being paid?" What consumers can expect to pay for online financial advising depends on the financial professional's experience and what the consumer is getting from the professional.

I personally recommend the Mint.com online money management software. It is free and pools all your accounts into one place so you can budget and see how you are doing. I also recommend Dave Ramsey's site (**www.daveramsey.com**) for people who are dealing with debt issues, and Morningstar® (**www.morningstar.com**) for investment research.

It is important for people to take an active role in the management of their personal finances because if they do not, their money will take over. Only you can be responsible for your future, and if you want financial security in that future, you must take control of your finances. If you do not put a plan in place today to be financially stable, then you have a very small chance of getting what you want in the long run. I am a big believer that your money and your life fulfillment are intertwined. It is hard to have either without being at peace with where the other is.

I would like to also mention that consumers should take caution in what they find on the Internet in regard to financial advice. Use common sense and approach most things with a skeptical, yet inquisitive attitude. There are many people with a blog or website about money who have no financial training and are trying to sell you something and/or scam you. Take what they say and go find the other side, and then you can make your own decision.

Online Asset Management

Do you know how much money you are worth? Your net worth is actually a different number than the amount of money you have sitting in your savings account. Your net worth is the amount of assets you have minus the amount of liabilities you have. Simply put, if you have $100,000 in the bank and owe $25,000 to various creditors, your net worth is $75,000. Of course, this is a highly simplified example — other factors should be considered, such as equity in real estate and other items such as investments, but knowing your net worth is important for a few reasons.

Knowing your net worth will give you a snapshot of where your finances stand right now and may also give you an idea of where you want to be financially. If you have a good deal of debt and not many assets, there is a good chance that you have a negative net worth as a result. Until you see this laid out in front of you, however, you may not recognize that you need to make some serious changes in the way you deal with your money.

Knowing your net worth is also helpful if you want to apply for a large loan, such as a mortgage loan or a loan to start a business. Lenders will want to know your net worth in order to decide whether you qualify for a loan. You can find many different net worth calculators online. Informational finance websites like Bankrate (**www.bankrate.com**) and Kiplinger (**http://kiplinger.com**) offer free net worth calculators that are easy to navigate and provide an estimate based on the information you provide. Many financial institutions offer these calculators as well. Regardless of which tool you choose to use, you will need to provide some information so the calculator can provide you with accurate results. Prepare to provide information regarding:

- The money you have in cash as well as in deposit accounts

- Money you have in retirement accounts, even if it is not accessible to you yet

- The value of any investments you have

- The amount of any cash-value life insurance policies in your name

- The value of your belongings, including the value of your primary residence (if you are the owner) as well as any other real estate

- The total amount of money you owe to any sources, including mortgages, loans, and revolving accounts

Most online net worth calculators will not only provide you with an estimate of your net worth, but will also offer advice to help you improve your net worth. The advice is general in nature and may be highly simplified — for example, it may suggest that you pay down your financial liabilities and save more money — but this can be helpful nonetheless.

Once you discover how much you are worth, it is time to determine how you should manage your money. This is another area where managing your money online can provide you with an abundance of options, many of them completely free.

Your financial institution might offer online tools as well as online consultations with financial advisers. This means that you might not need to visit the office of a financial adviser, but instead, you can conduct all your business using your computer; this is a convenient option if you are a busy person or simply do not like to make time for appointments.

You can also use the Internet to find and research a financial adviser. Once you find an adviser you want to use, check with the Better Business Bureau® (**www.bbb.org**) to read about any complaints filed against him or her. Next, find out if the adviser belongs to any professional organizations, and check out these organizations to make sure they are legitimate and reputable. To finish your research, conduct a general Internet search with the name of the financial adviser you are considering. This should uncover any complaints about the adviser that may have been posted on any of the consumer complaint websites. Sometimes these consumer complaints can be much more telling of a financial adviser's abilities — or inabilities — to handle customers' assets than the traditional means of the BBB. Do keep in mind, however, that the vast number of consumer complaint websites are not necessarily monitored, and therefore, there is no way to tell if the complaints are valid. Generally, though, if you find a huge number of complaints online about a certain wealth management adviser, this is probably a good indication that you will want to find someone else.

There is so much valuable information available online to help you managing your money that you may decide you can handle it on your own. Sometimes, this is indeed the case, but it takes dedication to successfully complete the task. If you have a great deal of assets, or if you are readying for a life change such as starting a family or preparing for retirement, financial advisers can be quite useful. Additionally, the right financial adviser can review your finances without any emotion involved. When you look at your money, you are emotionally invested in what you see, but a financial adviser can give you a frank analysis of your financial standing.

The bottom line is that you may not need a financial adviser, but you can probably benefit from a knowledgeable one who has your best interests in mind. Also be sure to explore the vast amounts of financial information available online while avoiding the not-so-credible sources. *The reliability of online financial information will be discussed in more detail in Chapter 13.*

Managing without an adviser

You can effectively manage your finances without a financial adviser if you take advantage of the many online tools available. You will need to keep in mind, however, that such online programs are automated systems that only look at your information from a computerized perspective. Some people, particularly those within the financial management field, may argue that though these financial management programs can be useful for basic money management tasks, they are in no way an adequate replacement for a qualified financial adviser who can take a broader look at your financial portfolio. A human financial adviser might be able to ask you questions that a computer program cannot and get more of a "feel" for your financial goals. If you do decide to manage your finances without the help of a professional adviser, or if you only plan on visiting an adviser once in a while, use the tools available to you on the Internet to not only keep your finances under control, but also to determine what you should be doing next with your money, whether it is increasing the amount of money you put into investments or aggressively paying down your mortgage.

Review the online resources available through your financial institution. Your bank, credit union, lenders, and insurance companies may offer a variety of financial management tools and resources free to customers. Some financial institutions offer free consultations with financial advisers. For example, USAA members can meet online or over the telephone with a financial adviser at no cost to find out if they are on the right track to eventually retire comfortably. These financial advisers are offered for the benefit of members, but also because a financial analysis may result in a recommendation for certain financial products offered through USAA, such as life insurance or additional retirement accounts. It is an opportunity for a customer to make sure his or her personal finances are stable, but it is also an opportunity for the financial institution to sell more products or services. Take advantage of such opportunities, but beware of advisers who may only push you to spend more money for the benefit of themselves and their company. If you feel as though the adviser is more concerned with getting you to buy something or sign up for a service than actually helping you, take a step back and do not sign anything until you have a had a chance to think things through and do some research.

If you decide to manage your finances solely with assistance from online tools and without the help of a financial adviser, you need to make sure that you are not concentrating too much on one aspect of your finances that you forget to deal with other important aspects of the total financial picture. For example, if you use an online budgeting tool along with an online spending log, you will likely have a great perspective on what your money is doing right now. On the other hand, if you forget to periodically review your investments (which you will learn more about in Chapter 9), or do not bother investing at all, your total financial portfolio will certainly be lacking. Although investing is not absolutely necessary for your financial health, it has the potential to build wealth in impressive ways.

When managing your finances yourself online, make sure you review all aspects of your finances, including:

- Your deposit accounts
- Your credit accounts
- Your investment accounts
- Your retirement accounts
- Your insurance policies

You will probably find that you have access to all of these accounts online, and in some instances, you can sign up for alerts when something important occurs, such as when a deposit hits your checking account or a stock you have invested in drops in value. Sign up for alerts by accessing your online accounts and looking for a link with wording similar to "Sign up for e-mail alerts" or "Sign up for mobile alerts."

How do you know what to do with your money once you have the ability to access all of your accounts online? Use some of the free calculators available online; they will reveal whether you have a balanced financial picture by assessing your current financial standing and then presenting simple recommendations. These calculators will ask you questions, such as what type of deposit accounts you have, how much insurance coverage you currently have, and what your net worth totals. The results you receive from these free online calculators are merely general advice, and if you have concerns about your finances, you should contact a financial professional. If you only need general advice as to whether you are handling your money as you should, then these free online calculators will help. You can find these calculators on your financial institutions' websites or through popular finance websites such as Bankrate (**www.bankrate.com**) or CNNMoney. com (**http://money.cnn.com**).

Managing when you are in financial trouble

Some might argue that having the "problem" of not knowing exactly what to do with all your money is not really a problem at all. There are many people who struggle to make ends meet and who must make difficult financial decisions, such as deciding whether to pay the electric bill or refill a prescription. The Internet can help these people as well, especially if people in this situation turn to a non-profit organization for help in lowering monthly payments.

If you find yourself behind in your bills, or quickly approaching a point where you might not be able to meet your financial obligations, you have the option to use the Internet to sign up for credit counseling. Some credit counseling services can simply help customers get their finances in order through budgeting tools and other programs, and some services operate as debt renegotiation programs. The credit counseling service you choose will work with your creditors to lower the amount of money you owe each month and will also counsel you on your money management habits. You can sign up for such a program online. Look for a non-profit credit counseling agency, such as American Consumer Credit Counseling (**www.consumercredit.com**), or search for a local counseling agency on the National Foundation for Credit Counseling website (**www.nfcc.org**). In most cases, you can sign up for credit counseling and manage your payment plan online. Take care to find the counseling agency through a credible source — such as the two sources listed above. There have been instances of credit counseling scams or agencies that were run so ineffectively that customers wound up in worse financial shape than they were when they first entered the program.

If your financial situation is truly dire and you are quickly running out of options, use the Internet to locate information regarding financial assistance programs for which you may qualify, such as rent assistance and reduced-cost or free medical care. You may be able to sign up for these programs using the Internet; otherwise, you should at least be able to make an appointment with someone at the agency through its website. For example, many welfare agencies will allow people to set up appointments online.

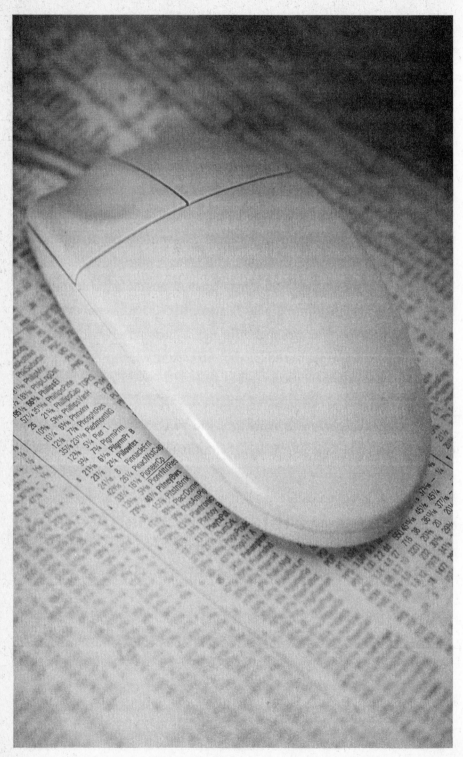

CHAPTER 6

BORROWING
MONEY ONLINE

The Internet is an incredibly useful tool when it comes to comparing a wide variety of lenders and credit products. In the past, consumers might check with a couple of lenders when applying for a credit product such as a credit card or loan or maybe three or four if they were determined to get the best deal. Consumers who wanted to aggressively pursue the very best interest rates and terms for credit products usually wound up seeking the services of a loan broker, who would accept a credit application on behalf of several potential lenders and determine which lender was willing to offer the best terms. Comparing several creditors used to be a time-consuming task, but this is not the case any longer.

Just as you can use the Internet the find the best sale price for boots, the lowest cost for a vacation, or even the best prices in town to buy groceries, you can use the same technology to find the best credit products. If you are envisioning going from one potential creditor's website to another in a labored attempt at finding the best interest rates and terms, do not worry: There are so many credit comparison websites that this is an unnecessary step. Finding out which creditor offers the best credit product you are looking for — such as a credit card or a loan — can be as easy as clicking a few buttons.

Why is it important to find the best interest rates and terms instead of simply assuming that your existing financial institution has the best offers? Even one or two interest rate percentage points can make a huge difference in the total amount of money you will pay over the life of a credit product, especially in the case of a loan with a long amortization such as a 15- or 30-year loan.

LEARN THE LINGO

Credit score: A three-digit number that is indicative of your credit history. The higher the score, the less of a credit risk you pose to creditors. The lower the score, the higher a credit risk you are, and you might be denied credit based on your poor credit history.

Credit report: A list of your credit history, as reported by your previous and present creditors. These reports are compiled and maintained by credit reporting agencies including Equifax, Experian, and TransUnion.

Credit reporting agencies: Companies that compile credit history information from creditors and then compile that information with previous data to assist potential creditors in ascertaining the risk of granting an individual consumer credit.

Fraud alert: An alert you place on your credit report when there has been an instance —or there is the potential for an instance — of identity theft or someone else has attempted to use your personal information.

Loan broker: An individual or website that accepts loan applications in an attempt to find the best loan product available.

Credit application: A document that presents questions and requests personal information in order to help a lender decide whether to extend credit to a potential borrower.

Interest rate: In credit products, a percentage of the amount you borrow that is charged by the lender to the consumer. In deposit accounts, a percentage of your balance that is credited toward your account.

Amortization: The gradual decrease in a total debt owed as a result of regularly scheduled payments.

Online Comparison "Shopping"

Before you start comparison shopping for credit products online, obtain a copy of your credit report to determine for which type of credit you will potentially qualify. For example, if you have a very low credit score, such as 520, then you should not bother applying for credit products that are advertised as only being available to people with excellent credit, which is defined by a FICO score of 800 and above. Additionally, if it is your intention to apply for a substantial amount of money, such as a home or car loan, then obtaining a copy of your credit report beforehand and fixing any errors or other problems on the report to raise your credit score might allow you to qualify for a lower interest rate and more favorable credit terms.

Request a free copy of your credit report annually at AnnualCreditReport. com (**www.annualcreditreport.com**). This is the only official website that provides you with the free annual credit report you are entitled to by law, but it will not provide you with a free copy of your credit score. Your credit report can tell you whether you have delinquent accounts or whether someone has stolen your identity and opened credit accounts in your name, but without paying an extra fee to see your credit score, you cannot determine what your specific score is. If you want to see your credit score, you will have to pay an extra fee. Similar websites may offer free copies of your credit report but will also require enrollment in a credit monitoring service or a similar program that will wind up costing you money.

You also have the option of requesting a copy of your credit report through any of the three major credit reporting agencies. Although these copies will cost money, the benefit is that you get to take a glimpse at your actual credit score:

- TransUnion (**www.transunion.com**)
- Equifax (**www.equifax.com**)
- Experian (**www.experian.com**)

If you are only interested in seeing your credit score, visit myFICO (**www. myfico.com**). Do take care when visiting any of these websites to only purchase what you intend to purchase. Almost all of these sites, although completely legitimate, will aggressively advertise the option to sign up for credit monitoring in return for a free copy of your credit report. Whether you should sign up for credit monitoring is up to you, but if you do not realize what you are actually signing up for you may be surprised to find a charge on your credit card statement after the initial free trial period. You might also find it difficult to cancel the membership if you do not keep a printed copy of the confirmation you received when you first signed up for the free trial.

A credit monitoring service is an automated service that monitors your credit report and alerts you when anything occurs that might indicate fraud of some sort, including a new account opened or a credit application submitted. This service will also alert you when changes occur on your credit report that may impact your credit score, such as inquiries, drops or increases in your credit score, or new accounts opened. If you frequently worry that someone has stolen your identity, this type of service can offer you piece of mind. On the other hand, most consumers do just fine with simply reviewing their credit reports annually or every six months to make sure suspicious activity has not occurred.

Once you know your credit score, you should have a good idea of the type of credit for which you may qualify. Though a credit score is not the sole item most lenders examine when deciding whether to approve a credit application, many of the credit comparison websites will list the type of credit each particular lender is looking for, whether it is fair, good, excellent, or a subprime credit product marketed specifically to consumers with very low credit scores. Knowing what you qualify for will allow you to apply for the highest level — in other words, the lowest interest rates and best terms — of credit without wasting your time applying for credit you cannot qualify for based on your credit score. Each time you apply for a new credit account, whether it is a credit card or a loan, a notation is placed on your credit report. These inquiries, which occur when a creditor reviews your credit report in an attempt to decide whether your application will be approved or denied, can actually drag your credit score down if you have too many of them, so avoid applying for credit products unless you are fairly sure that you will actually be approved.

The following is a short list of some of the credit comparison websites that offer a long list of creditors. Also included on each site is the credit scale each individual creditor looks for and the location of each creditor:

- Bankrate (**www.bankrate.com**)

- CreditCards.com (**www.creditcards.com**)

- BANKS.com (**www.banks.com**)

- CardRatings.com (**www.cardratings.com**)

After you find the creditor that most appeals to you based on the credit terms offered, you may have the option of clicking on a link that will take you directly to a credit application Web page. Although this is certainly a convenient option, it is usually a better idea to go directly to the official website of the creditor. There are a couple of reasons for this: You want to first verify that the interest rates and terms listed on the comparison website were accurate because sometimes the information is outdated or simply wrong, and also you want to ensure that your application for credit does not fall into the wrong hands. Because your application contains important information, including your social security number and other sensitive data, applying directly through the creditor's official website makes the transfer of information safer than if you send it through a comparison website.

Applying for Credit

You will be hard pressed to find a creditor that is unwilling to accept a credit application online. The process of accepting and processing a credit application through the Internet is much less expensive and time-consuming than accepting an application over the phone, through the mail, or in person. For this reason, if you want to apply for any type of credit — credit cards, loans, lines of credit, or mortgages — there is an excellent chance that you will be able to do so using the Internet.

You already know that applying for credit should be accomplished directly on the official website of the creditor. In some instances, when you attempt to apply for credit through the official website, you will be redirected to another website to actually fill out the application. This is a common occurrence, especially with credit cards, because the website offering the credit card often is not the creditor who actually makes the decision. For example, if you want to apply for a Toys "R" Us® MasterCard® credit card and begin your search on the official Toys "R" Us website (**www.toysrus. com**), when you click the button to apply for the credit card, your Internet browser session will be redirected to the official Chase® website because this is the company that actually owns the Toys "R" Us MasterCard accounts.

Do pay attention to where you are redirected, though. If you are filling out a credit card application through one website but suddenly find your Internet session redirected to another website in the middle of your session, a site that does not appear to have any legitimate reason to request your private information, there is a chance it is a fraudulent attempt to obtain your personal financial information. Trust your instincts. If you cannot shake the feeling that there is something wrong with the online application process, stop the process, close the browser session, and run a virus scan before you try again. If you experience the same problem a second time, contact customer support to make sure you are on the right track before you proceed.

Credit cards, car loans, and personal loans

A great feature often offered along with online credit applications is an instant decision on your application. Creditors can offer this feature through their websites, because the credit decision process is largely computerized.

There is not a human loan officer sitting at a desk somewhere and reviewing credit applications as they arrive via the Internet. Instead, a computer program quickly analyzes the information contained on your application as well as the data contained on your credit report. If you qualify for approval based on this information, you will receive a message that you are approved.

Different websites handle the approval notification process differently. Some will send an e-mail to you to let you know whether or not your application was approved, but others will instruct you to refresh the Web page after a certain period of time for the credit decision to appear. If you receive an approval, the notification will provide you with further instructions regarding the steps to take in order to access the account. If your credit application is denied, you will receive notification that the creditor was unable to approve you at that time. You will also be informed that you will receive a letter through postal mail explaining the reasons your application was denied. This letter is required of all creditors when they deny an application, and it entitles you to a free copy of your credit report so you can see why the application was denied.

In some instances, the creditor cannot offer you an instant approval. Sometimes, the approval process is delayed due to computer issues or because the credit review software is not working. Sometimes, however, the creditor simply needs additional time to review the information you have submitted in your credit application. In this instance, the creditor should notify you as to when you can expect a decision. This decision might be delivered via e-mail or postal mail. Additionally, if you have a fraud alert placed on your credit report, online applications for credit will not be instantly approved because the creditor must first verbally verify that you are indeed the person applying for the credit, not someone else posing as you.

If you want to apply for a car loan online and already have a specific car in mind, be sure that you have information for the vehicle handy when you fill out the loan application. You will want to have the make, model, and year of the car as well as the vehicle identification number (VIN) unique to the car. Of course, if you are attempting to fill out a loan application online in the hopes of being preapproved, you will not yet have this information. However, if you do know which car you want to buy, or if you are trying to refinance a loan for a car you already own, having this information when you fill out the online loan application should speed up the process. Remember: You do not have to obtain your car loan through the dealership, even if you are buying a brand new car. If your bank or credit union offers better rates, get a loan through your financial institution instead of financing from the dealership.

Applying for a loan or credit card online is usually a very simple process. The following steps are general instructions, as the specific procedures vary by creditor:

1. Visit the website for the creditor and click on the link for "Apply."

2. Complete the application by providing all the requested information including contact information, income data, and any other information needed by the creditor.

3. Submit the application when completed. Some financial institutions will require additional information, such as copies of pay stubs or tax returns. The financial institution will alert you if other documentation is required.

4. You will either receive notification of the application decision (approval or denial) immediately or will receive notification that the application will take a certain amount of time to process.

Credit applications vary, but the important thing to remember is to fill them out as completely and accurately as possible.

LEARN THE LINGO

Vehicle identification number: Also referred to as a VIN, this is the unique string of numbers and letters assigned to every vehicle.

Preapproval: The approval of a specific loan amount in order for the consumer to give an offer to purchase something, commonly for a car or home. Preapprovals have already received credit approval, but can be subject to additional stipulations before the loans funds will actually be released.

Preapprovals

Sometimes creditors will send out notifications to customers — through the postal mail or e-mail — informing them that they have been preapproved for a credit product, which may include credit cards or loans. You may also notice a link relating to a preapproved credit card or loan preapproval on your financial institution's website when accessing your deposit or credit accounts. These preapprovals are usually the result of a preliminary review of your credit report and are still considered "approved upon final credit approval." This means that even though your credit report appears to point to your creditworthiness, the creditor may still require some additional information to fully approve you, such as income or employment verification. So, though sometimes all the creditor needs is your go-ahead to open the credit account or issue the loan, other times, a preapproval can result in a denied credit application.

Depending on the creditor, you can sometimes apply for preapprovals online. Find out if your preferred creditor offers online preapprovals by checking its website or speaking to a customer service representative.

Be extremely leery of random preapprovals you encounter while browsing the Internet. Banners, pop-ups, and e-mails from creditors you have no affiliation with should be ignored, even if these notifications assure you that you have been preapproved for a very attractive credit product. If you enter personal information for such a product, you run the risk of your private information being sent somewhere other than where you think it is going. For this reason, do not respond to a preapproval from a lender with which you are not familiar. If the credit product seems incredibly appealing and you want to pursue this preapproval opportunity, do not utilize the link sent to you through the pop-up or e-mail. Instead, go directly to the official website for the creditor and apply there. If you have never heard of the creditor, and when you attempt to find the official website for the creditor you cannot find it or the website seems a little "off," do not submit personal information with that lender until you can verify its legitimacy.

If your credit application is approved, you might be required to supply some form of documentation, such as a copy of your identification card, a savings account statement, or a copy of your pay statement from your employer, before the loan funds will be disbursed or the credit card will be issued. If you have a scanner, ask a representative from the creditor if you can send the documents via e-mail. This will speed up the process much faster than mailing copies via the U.S. Postal Service. It will also reduce the likelihood of the documents being lost in the mail or winding up in the wrong hands. Faxing is also an option, but do ask the financial representative if the faxed documents will go directly to his or her desk or will instead be handled by many people. The fewer people with access to your personal financial information, the better.

If you encounter any problems during the credit application process, look on the creditor's website for a link to customer support. You may be able to find the answers to your questions in the FAQ section of the website. If the FAQ does not answer your question, you may be able to speak with a customer service representative via online chat or through e-mail. If all else fails, call the phone number listed on the website.

LEARN THE LINGO

Closing: An event during the process of buying a home where all mortgage documents are signed and ownership of the home is transferred to the new owners.

P2P lending: Peer-to-peer lending, which involves lending between individuals or groups of people with no involvement from a formal lending institution. One example of P2P lending is a loan between two friends.

Social lending websites: Websites that assist individuals or groups in finding lenders or borrowers. This is a common platform for P2P lending.

Down payment: A payment made toward a loan when the loan is initially obtained. Examples include down payments for homes and for cars.

Mortgage loan applications

Applying for a mortgage loan is different than applying for other types of credit; although, most mortgage lenders still offer the option of filling out the application online. Though most mortgage lenders will provide prequalifications online, it is a preapproval you actually want because this tells sellers that you have already been through the loan process and are approved pending the selection of the home for purchase. When completing a mortgage loan application, be prepared for a few things:

- The application process is lengthy. You will be asked a wide variety of questions about almost every aspect of your personal finances. For this reason, most mortgage lenders offer applicants the option of saving loan applications and returning to them later for completion.

- The process is not completely automated. Though a computer program will probably review your application and credit score, and though you may be offered a preliminary approval, every mortgage application is reviewed by a human at some point before it goes to closing.

- You will have to supply a great deal of documentation for most mortgage loans, such as proof of income, tax returns, and bank statements.

- There are additional steps to most mortgage loans that cannot be accomplished online, including a home appraisal and survey.

You can begin the process of applying for a mortgage loan online, and most mortgage lenders try to make as much of the process as Internet-friendly as possible because it is convenient for customers and it can speed up the entire process exponentially. Due to the special nature of a mortgage loan, it is not feasible for the process of obtaining a mortgage loan to occur completely over the Internet. Preapprovals are available online, but there are simply too many required document verifications to allow an instant approval over the Internet for this type of loan.

If your mortgage application is for a home that you have already chosen, do a quick check of the home's market value before you apply. You want to make sure that the home is not being sold for more than it is actually worth, because this will surely result in a denial of the application. A good online source for checking the market values of homes is Zillow. com (**www.zillow.com**). This is a fairly reliable, up-to-date website that can provide you with a free estimated market value for a home based on the street address you provide. County websites may also offer valuable information regarding the home you want to purchase, including the tax assessment value and the amount of money the home was purchased for by the current owners. Review all this information online before you begin the mortgage application process.

Applying for a mortgage loan is similar to the process of applying for other types of loans; although, a mortgage loan application will be lengthier. Access the online application through the lender's website and fill out the application completely. After you submit the application you will receive instructions regarding the next step, whether it is picking out a home or contacting a representative to supply documentation.

CASE STUDY: FINDING MORTGAGE HELP ONLINE

Casey, personal trainer

I recently had my mortgage loan holder changed because my mortgage was sold to another servicer. Initially, I was irritated and stressed out because I was not able to contact them because the customer service number listed on the notification they sent me through the mail was not even in service yet. The notification they sent me stated my loan was purchased by them and it included different phone numbers to contact them, but the main number had a message saying it was not in service. It was incredibly frustrating because I wanted to make sure my mortgage payment would not be late, but I could not get in contact with my new mortgage loan holder using the information they had provided me. With my work schedule, I do not have much time to search for a phone number and stress about my mortgage.

I decided to go online to find a different phone number for this loan company to get in contact with them. I found one through their website and eventually was able to contact them and received all the information I needed on my mortgage loan. What a relief! I am glad I checked online to find a different number so I could stop worrying about it. Besides, I am now aware that loans change hands between lenders quite frequently, and it is nothing to get worked up about. If I had not been able to go online and find out all this information I probably would have been in a panic about the whole situation.

Loan brokers

Loan brokers are available for a variety of loans, but are most commonly utilized for mortgages. These professionals accept an application for credit on behalf of several lenders and find the best deal for the applicant. Though some brokers charge applicants for this service, other brokers make their money by charging a fee to the lenders. Some websites, such as Lending-

Tree (**www.lendingtree.com**), act as loan brokers by accepting applications online and distributing the applicant's information to a variety of lenders; in this instance, a human broker does not send out the application. This is merely an automated service conducted solely online by software. Submit an application through one of these websites just as you would for a creditor; respond to all the application questions thoroughly and click "submit."

You can choose to work with a human loan broker rather than an automated system and still conduct your business mainly via the Internet. Find a broker by searching online, flipping through a local phone book, or obtaining a personal recommendation from someone you know. Many loan brokers are eager to conduct business over the Internet because it simplifies the process and saves them time as well. Alternatively, you can choose to utilize a loan comparison website to act as a broker. Examples of such loan comparison websites include Quicken Loans (**www.quickenloans.com**) and LendingTree (**www.lendingtree.com**). The benefit to using a broker or comparison websites is that you do not have to do all the comparison shopping for the best interest rate yourself; instead, it is accomplished for you. The downside to these types of services is that you can never be entirely sure that the pool of lenders the broker or website deals with actually has the best interest rates and terms. If you are not comfortable with the idea of a large group of lenders gaining access to your personal information, these services are not for you. However, if you want to aggressively pursue the best loan, a broker or comparison website can be a great tool to assist you.

Peer-to-peer lending

The Internet has taken the concept of peer-to-peer lending, also called P2P lending, to an entirely new level. P2P involves lending between two individuals or groups of individuals rather than a financial institution. Although borrowing money from another individual when a suitable loan cannot be obtained by traditional means is certainly nothing new, online resources take the concept of people lending funds to other people and makes it big business.

Family and friends

Do you want to lend money to your nephew but are afraid that he will not pay you back in a timely manner? Do you want to borrow money from your friend but are afraid that a financial transaction might sour the close relationship the two of you have? The Internet has a solution for these problems: social lending websites.

A social lending site acts as an intermediary between two people conducting a financial transaction. The borrower and the lender agree to the terms of the loan, and the website takes care of the details that might not otherwise be covered if the loan agreement is merely conducted over a handshake. A great example of this type of site is Virgin Money (**www.virginmoneyus. com**). This social lending website offers a variety of services online:

- Virgin Money will take the loan information from the borrower and lender and compose a legally binding promissory note.

- Virgin Money will also grant both the lender and borrower access to loan information online. The lender can review loan information using the website, and the borrower can use the website to make payments to the loan.

- If the borrower defaults on the loan, it is Virgin Money that contacts him or her and assesses a late fee. This saves the lender and the borrower from involving themselves in a potentially awkward conversation.

Websites such as Virgin Money do charge a fee for their services. The fee is usually comparable to — or less than — what would be paid to an attorney to handle the details of the loan. Additionally, this website offers advice for loan situations that might result in additional tax considerations. For example, a minimum interest rate must be charged for loans of certain amounts; otherwise, the IRS considers the loan a gift. The real benefit to using this type of website when lending money to someone you know, or borrowing money from someone you know, is that the relationship has a potentially better chance of staying intact because it is a third party that handles all the monetary details.

What do you do if you do not qualify for a loan through a financial institution and you do not personally know anyone willing to lend you money? The Internet offers some interesting options in the form of P2P lending websites.

These websites are relatively simple to use. You register on the website as either a lender or a borrower. If you are a lender — sometimes called an "investor" by some websites — you can browse through the vast database of potential borrowers. Some of the borrowers post pictures of themselves and explain why they need the money. If you register as a borrower, you may have to agree to a credit report review that will be accessible to potential lenders, sometimes in the form of a credit rating unique to the website. For example, a star rating might be given to borrowers, with the number of starts relating to their creditworthiness. For example, a borrower with excellent credit might be given five stars, while a borrower with very bad credit might only be given one star. These ratings can be based on an actual credit score combined with loan repayment history from the actual website.

Although the various P2P lending websites operate differently, the format is basically the same. Borrowers issue an appeal for a loan, and interested lenders commit to providing some, or all, of the loan amount. The website handles composing loan documents, collecting payments from borrowers, distributing payments to lenders, and taking any other necessary steps.

This is an option for people who cannot get a loan through traditional means and who are willing to ask for a loan from strangers. It is also an option for people who want to try their hands at lending money, either for profit, by charging interest for the loan, or simply because they want to help people.

If this concept interests you, either as a borrower or as a lender, the following is a short list of some of the most popular P2P websites:

- **Prosper (www.prosper.com)**: An online lending community for people who want to borrow or lend money. Borrowers can list loan requests between $1,000 and $25,000.

- **Lending Club (www.lendingclub.com)**: An online lending community where borrowers and investors are brought together to benefit financially.

- **Kiva (www.kiva.org)**: A website that gives investors the opportunity to lend money to people in developing countries to help them build their own businesses.

Using a website that is specific to P2P lending is a far better idea than some of the alternatives. For example, you do not want to hop onto an online classified ad website and place an ad asking for a lender or answering an ad for someone asking for a loan. There are simply too many potential problems that can arise when you get into a situation like this. You cannot know if the other person you deal with is genuine. How can you be sure that the person you lend money to will pay you back or if that person is even who he or she claims to be? If you are borrowing money, how can you be sure that the other person will not suddenly start making demands for a higher interest rate or fees that you never agreed to? A website that not only takes steps to verify the borrowers' and lenders' identities as well as takes care of the documentation involved with the loan is the best choice. This is not to say that potential problems do not exist with established lending websites, but choosing one that offers safeguards can minimize these risks.

Should you lend money online? It is one thing to use online services to set up a loan between you and someone you know, but it is another thing to be a lender for a website that pairs you with complete strangers who need a loan. You can make money as a lender — especially if you command a high interest rate for the money you lend — but there can be a great deal of risk involved with this type of transaction. If you do decide to lend money using a social lending website, only use money that you can spare. Do not empty your savings account in order to load funds onto the website, and do not count on the money you will make to pay your bills. You must be willing to accept some degree of financial risk when you become a social borrowing lender, but you can take matters into your own hands by personally selecting who you will lend money to through the website.

Estimate Debt Payments

You do not have to guess — or even speak with a customer service representative — when determining what your potential monthly payment will be on a loan you are considering. In fact, you do not have to have much specific information in order to get an estimated payment. If you know how much money you want to borrow, the interest rate, and the number of months over which you will pay back your loan, you can get a very close estimate of what your monthly payment will be. Sometimes, the estimate will be within a dollar or two of the actual monthly payment, but this depends on aspects such as lender fees, down payments, and interest rates, which might change the total amount you owe.

Why should you care about getting an estimate for a loan payment before you even apply? There are a number of reasons why you should utilize the Internet to estimate a loan payment including:

- You can figure out how much your monthly payment will be based on several scenarios, such as the length of the loan or the total amount borrowed. This can be helpful if you know how much money you are willing to spend each month for the payment because you can change the figures to suit your budget. You can compare different loan offers to determine which one will give you the best overall deal. For example, a lower interest rate can be attractive, but if you are looking for the lowest monthly payment, a loan that has a longer amortization might be the best choice.

- You can decide whether you will need to make a down payment in order to obtain the monthly loan payment you want. This can be an important factor when getting a car loan in particular, especially if you have a high credit score and the option of buying the car without making a down payment.

You can find free calculators on most websites that are dedicated to financial information including Bankrate.com and Banks.com. You should never pay to access a payment calculator, nor should you ever provide your credit card information to a website that purports to offer free access to a payment calculator tool yet claims to need your credit card number for verification or something similar. This is one instance where you can obtain the information you need free of charge and without supplying any personal identifying information. In most cases, you can simply go straight to the payment calculator directly from another link and input your information.

Payment estimates

What type of information will you need to provide to get an estimate of what your monthly loan payment will be? The amount of information you will have to provide depends on the calculator. If you use a loan payment calculator on your lender's official website, the interest rate and some other information may be prefilled by the website. This can save you a little time because you will not have to search for information about the expected interest rate.

It is important to note that using an online payment calculator — even if it is directly through your lender's website — does not guarantee a loan, a certain interest rate, or specific loan terms. These calculators are great tools and are offered as a courtesy, but they should always be considered estimates. An exact monthly payment usually is not final until you receive written confirmation of the details of your loan. In other words, you cannot assume that just because a lender's payment calculator pre-fills with a certain interest rate that this is the interest rate you will receive. Some lenders offer different interest rates depending on an applicant's creditworthiness, so if you have a few blemishes on your credit report you may not be offered the low interest rate predominantly advertised on the lender's website, which will probably be the default interest rate pre-filled into the online payment calculator. If you are not sure whether your lender offers different interest rates to different applicants based on credit scores and other qualifying factors, check the website for a link to the lender's interest rates for loans. All the interest rates should be listed on the website, or at the very least, there should be a note directing interested applicants to speak to a customer service representative regarding variations in interest rates.

Find an online calculator that is specific to the type of loan that you intend on obtaining. Some loans, such as mortgage loans, have additional factors, such as taxes and insurance, that must be taken into consideration when estimating the monthly payment.

Some calculators may ask for additional information to give you a more comprehensive view of what your monthly payment might be. For example, some online calculators will give you the option to adjust the figures and see how much you might save overall by choosing a shorter amortization, providing a down payment, or making additional payments consistently or as a one-time payment.

This is one of the greatest advantages of online payment calculators; you can adjust with the numbers to determine which scenario works best for your situation. Suppose you know that you want to have a car loan payment less than $200 per month. With this number in mind, you can determine the total amount you should spend when buying the car. If you find a car that is perfect for you — except that the sale price is a little more money than you had planned to spend, you can use an online payment calculator to change your scenario. Maybe you will stretch the length of the loan out another year or two, or perhaps you will consider making a down payment in order to get the car you really want without exceeding your monthly budget.

Using the Internet in this way can take a lot of the guesswork out of getting a loan. In the past, most people had to meet with a loan officer to determine the various loan payment options available. Today, with the help of the Internet, this task can be accomplished without setting foot into a loan officer's office.

Online calculators can also help you make other important financial decisions:

- Should you buy a car, or should you lease a car? This type of calculator will show you which option makes more sense for your financial situation.

- Should you make extra payments? These calculators will show you how much money in interest you can save in the long term by making extra payments, either as one-time payments or regular monthly payments along with your regularly scheduled payment.

- What type of loan should you choose? Some calculators will help you examine whether a rebate from the car dealership is better than a lower interest car loan, or vice versa.

These are the type of questions a loan officer can help you answer, but why bother making an appointment to speak to a loan officer when you can get this information on your own using the Internet? You can find calculators for all of the above questions at Bankrate.com.

Payment estimator for refinancing

You can find out whether it is worth it to refinance by using an online payment calculator. A lower interest rate is not the only consideration when deciding whether to refinance a loan, especially when the loan features closing costs and other fees. By using a calculator, you can determine whether a refinance will save you money or actually cost you money in the end.

It is also a good idea to use an online calculator if you are thinking about consolidating your debt into one loan. You will want to determine whether the consolidation will lower your monthly payment significantly and whether any fees associated with the consolidation will be quickly absorbed by the interest rate savings you will enjoy.

Refinancing calculators will compare the current loan you have with a new loan. For this reason, you will need to provide the details of your current loan. Log on to your account to find out your current balance, interest rate, and remaining loan term to make sure the information you input into the online calculator is as accurate as possible. You can also use specific online calculators that are designed to estimate closing costs if the refinance is for a mortgage. Look for these calculators on your financial institution's website or a website such as Bankrate.com or Mortgage Calculator (**www. mortgagecalculator.org**).

CHAPTER 7

ONLINE SHOPPING & SAVING MONEY

If you are an avid shopper — or if you are passionate about making sure that you do not spend more money than you should when making purchases — you will soon find that the Internet is a fantastic tool. In fact, if you are the type of person who seeks out deals and discounts, and you do not yet use the Internet to assist you, then you are missing out. Comparison shopping, finding sales, and making sure that you do not pay full price for items you can get at a discount are just a few of the great features you will find online.

Comparison Shopping

Comparison shopping used to involve combing through the ads in the Sunday paper to find out which store was offering the lowest prices on a particular item. Although this is still an option for people who actually enjoy sifting through printed ads, you can save a great deal of time by using the Internet as a source for finding the lowest prices on the items you want to buy.

Can you actually save money by using the Internet to compare prices? Consider a website such as GasBuddy.com, which allows you to input your ZIP code to find out which gas station near you is offering the lowest prices on gasoline. If you use your car quite a bit or if gas prices have gone up significantly, knowing which gas station sells the cheapest gas is necessary before heading out to fill up your tank. When you consider this and other websites such as GroceryGuide.com and MyPlanRate.com (for cell phones), you will soon understand that comparison shopping online is not confined to only items traditionally bought online. Comparison shopping can be done using the Internet for items you intend to purchase in-store. You choose whether to use a comparison website — such as the websites mentioned above — or if you would rather check websites for several merchants in order to find the best prices. Either way, using the Internet will save you time from driving from store to store in an attempt to find the best price.

Do not discount the idea of buying things online. Many items can be purchased online for less than they cost in a traditional store. Some stores also offer the option to purchase items at special Internet prices and have the item shipped directly to a store location close to the buyer so shipping and handling charges can be avoided. So, if the lowest price is online, but you do not want to pay extra to have the item shipped to you, there are alternatives. Many websites also offer free shipping, either sporadically or regularly.

How can you tell whether the item you want to purchase is offered for less online than it is in-store? One easy way to tell is by noting the cost of items during your next shopping trip and comparing the prices for the same items on another merchant's website. Retailers such as Target, Wal-Mart, and Sears offer merchandise both in-store and online, so look at the store's website to find out whether you can buy the items cheaper by buying online. There is a good chance that you will find that at least a few of the items you regularly buy cost less when ordered online.

Coupons and More

You can find plenty of information online, but when your goal is to find ways to save money, use the Internet to make sure that you are not paying full price.

Take a look at the following websites the next time you make a purchase online:

- RetailMeNot (**www.retailmenot.com**)
- CouponCabin (**www.couponcabin.com**)
- CouponHeaven.com (**www.couponheaven.com**)
- DealCatcher (**www.dealcatcher.com**)

These and other websites provide information about getting good deals and finding sales, but more importantly they provide online coupon codes for a wide variety of merchants. Coupon codes are the codes customers can use to receive discounts for online purchases, usually for a percentage off the total purchase or a set discount amount such as $5 off a $50 purchase.

If you have purchased something online, you might already be familiar with coupon codes and where customers enter them on most websites. When finalizing your purchase, you are brought to a virtual checkout screen where you provide your credit card number, shipping address, and any other information needed by the merchant. The area where customers enter the coupon code is usually a box that asks for a coupon code, discount code, promotional code, or something similar. By entering a valid coupon code, you purchase the item for less than the full price.

Merchants often send coupon codes to customers who are on the merchant's e-mail listing. Coupon code websites publish these coupon codes, making the codes available to everyone who searches for them on the Internet.

Here is an example of how you might search for and use a coupon code. Suppose you want to purchase an item from Amazon.com. Before you make your purchase, you use a search engine to look for a coupon code by typing "Amazon coupon codes" in the search engine's search feature. The search engine will probably give several options, allowing you to search through the websites to find a valid coupon code that is suitable for the item you intend to buy. Although not all coupon codes listed on these sites are valid because they are frequently provided by other visitors and may be expired or simply not real, if you can find a coupon code that works for your purchase, you will save money. Sometimes, coupon codes are a word, while other times, it is a mixture of letters, number, or a combination of both. Pay close attention to capitalization because some coupon code boxes are case sensitive.

If you do not have a coupon code, take a look at the main page of the merchant's website before you begin adding items to your virtual cart. There may be a coupon code or discount advertised right on the main Web page that will save you money. Do not forget to take a look for a tab or link that says "Sale," or "Clearance Items," because these sections often contain deeply discounted items.

LEARN THE LINGO

Case sensitive: This refers to codes or passwords that must be entered in the exact form it was originally created, including correct use of capitalization and spacing. For example, the code "H2ff" would not work if entered as "h2FF."

Loan officer: A representative from a lender who assists applicants and makes credit decisions, often in conjunction with automated lending software.

Coupon codes: A series of letters and/or numbers that can be used during an online checkout to receive a discount.

Online auctions: Websites offering items for sale, allowing potential buyers to bid on how much they are willing to pay. The item goes to the highest bidder.

Bidding war: In an online auction environment, when potential buyers compete against each other to make the highest bid in order to obtain the item offered.

PayPal: A website that allows users to transfer money to other users or make secure online payments.

Coupons for printing

Clipping coupons from a newspaper is one way to save money, but today, it is possible to look for a coupon online, print it, and take it to a local merchant to receive a discount. The coupons usually feature Universal Product Code (UPC), which is a barcode featuring specific numbers for specific items, and other information commonly found on coupons in newspapers, magazines, and mailings. Online coupons are offered by the websites for manufacturers as well as directly from websites for merchants. Online coupons make sense for manufacturers and merchants because they cost less money to produce — after all, the customers pay to print the coupons, not the merchant or manufacturer — and there is also a better chance of the coupon being seen by more people via e-mails and social networking websites, such as Facebook and Twitter. Online coupons are often shared among friends and family.

Internet sales

Many merchants offer special pricing for items purchased online. Often, these are called "Internet-only" specials. This means that the special discounted price is only available if you purchase the item over the Internet rather that in the store. Sometimes, Internet-only discounts are so substantial that if you are considering an in-store purchase, it is definitely worth looking at the merchant's website to see if such a savings is available — especially if you are buying a high-ticket item. In some instances, you do not have to actually make the purchase online, but you do have to print a copy of the online ad to present to the salesperson. This is a tactic some merchants use to compel people to go from simply looking at the website to actually taking action and making the purchase, such as with car dealerships or furniture stores.

Here is an example. Customer A walks into a local car dealership and negotiates the price of a car. She gets a fairly good deal but has to spend a couple of hours in the haggling process. Customer B spends a little time on the Internet beforehand and finds out which dealership is offering the best deal on the type of car she wants. She then negotiates the price of the car with a salesperson via e-mail without even stepping foot into the dealership. To make the scenario even better, she begins with a lower asking price from the dealership because she found an Internet special offered on the dealership's website and winds up paying far less than Customer A as a result.

Not only can you find a lower price for some items by researching purchases online, but once in a while, you can find bonuses online that are not advertised in the store. These are additional discounts or bonus items given to a customer with a purchase. One example is car dealerships offering free television sets or tickets for weekend getaways with the purchase of a car. Furniture stores sometimes offer similar deals by giving something away, such as a lamp or a TV, when a larger item is purchased, such as a living room set, but only when the customer presents a printed coupon from the Internet.

You may not always get the best price by purchasing online. Instead, use the Internet to research purchases to find out where you can get the best deal. After all, effectively managing your personal finances involves making sure that you are not spending too much on the items you buy.

Online Auctions

Online auction websites can be likened to a virtual flea market; users present items for sale by posting photos and descriptions of the items on the website, and other users can browse the offerings and purchase the items. You can find some really great deals on these websites, potentially saving you quite a bit of money compared to what you would pay shopping elsewhere. Although some items are offered for a non-negotiable price, others are presented for a certain price for a certain amount of time, and users place bids depending on how much money they are willing to spend to purchase the project. The user who bids the most money before the bidding period ends is able to buy the item.

Online auctions offer a simplified format and the ability to post several photographs and descriptions of the item for sale. There is also a potential for a higher profit if the item results in a bidding war, which involves two or more bidders competing against each other to offer the highest bid in an attempt to obtain the item being sold. However, there is almost always a fee for presenting items on Internet auctions, and sometimes, the effort put forth by the seller to present the item to buyers is not worth the price the item eventually sells for.

If you have not yet ventured into the realm of online auctions, you should know the following information:

- You may be able to buy items at substantially reduced prices.
- You can make extra money by selling items.
- It is really easy to get carried away.

Online auction websites such as eBay or WeBidz allow members to buy and sell items online. The allure of online auctions varies depending on the users. Some people like the rare items they can find using online auctions, but other people truly enjoy the thrill of winning a bidding war for an item.

The bidding process is what makes these websites so intriguing for many people. A seller puts an item up for sale and sets a starting price. Prospective buyers who are registered on the website then bid on the item. With items that are in demand, the bidding process can become quite competitive with hopeful buyers submitting bid after bid in an attempt to outbid other bidders and become the "winner" of the item. Some winning bidders wind up in a bit of financial trouble after having spent far more than they anticipated because they were caught up in bidding wars and failed to keep the purchase in perspective. If you use online auction websites and find yourself thinking more about winning the item rather than finding the best deal, you may want to step away from the auction website until you are able to purchase items without getting carried away. For some people, simply staying away from the auction websites completely is the best option.

Of course, there are plenty of people who successfully utilize online auctions for both buying and selling and who never wind up getting carried away. Consider online auctions as a means by which to sell items you no longer need or want or bring in a side income, but be sure to read all of the terms and conditions on the website before posting your item for sale. You will probably find that you have to pay a fee even if the item never sells. You may also wind up selling the item for far less than it is worth if not many users bid on the item. Remember that online auction purchases are considered legal agreements, so you cannot simply decide to not sell an item because you did not get a high enough bid nor can you back out of purchasing an item simply because you experience buyer's remorse.

If you have items you would like to sell online, but do not want to deal directly with auction websites, you can choose to utilize the services of someone who sells items online professionally. Find these services by searching through your local phone book or online. These people earn money by taking a percentage of your profit from the item you sell. You also have the option of placing a classified ad online in an attempt to sell your items using a website such as Craigslist or the online version of your local newspaper's classified ads, which should be available on your local newspaper's website.

Items that are difficult to ship or must be seen up close to really be appreciated — such as art or collectibles — may not sell very well on eBay and other auction websites. Also, even though you might be able to get an astounding deal on big-ticket items such as an automobile using an auction website, you will need determine whether making this purchase before viewing the item is worth the risk. When buying or selling something of considerable value — or something that should be inspected prior to the completion of the transaction — use an escrow agent such as Escrow.com to hold the funds in an account while you inspect the item. You should verify that the item received is the same as the item purchased. The escrow website will charge a fee for this service, but for expensive items, the fee is usually worth the service and helps ensure both buyer and seller are satisfied.

Shopping Online Safely

Although it is certainly true that you can find great deals online, it is also unfortunately true that it is possible to run into problems when shopping online. Buying items online is different from making your purchases in person at a store. You cannot see who is actually selling you the items and you cannot reach out and touch the items to make sure they are exactly what you wanted to purchase. You also have no way of knowing whether the person processing your credit card payment is then passing that information along to other people for criminal use. These are just some of the reasons why many people avoid shopping online. Credit card fraud and identity theft can certainly occur online, but by taking some precautions and making common-sense decisions, you can keep your information safe while managing to save quite a bit of money on the items you buy:

- **Take the time to read the fine print**. You might get so excited about finding the exact item you were looking for at a great price that you forget to look at the shipping and handling charges. Sometimes merchants offer rock-bottom prices for items to lure in customers, but then turn charge an exorbitant amount of money for shipping and handling.

- **Never input your credit card number on a website if you are not planning to make a purchase**. A good example of this includes websites that offer free copies of your credit report. You might figure that providing your credit card number is reasonable because it might be used as a form of identification. If you do not read the fine print, you might later realize that your credit card has been charged monthly for a credit monitoring service.

- **Know who you are dealing with**. If you find an item you would like to purchase on a website you have never done business with before — or have never even heard of — make sure the payment transaction process is secure by looking for "https" instead of "http" in the Web address of the payment screen. It may also be worth your time to do a quick Internet search to see if there are any complaints about the merchant online; an online merchant that does not deliver goods as promised or who overcharges customers is bound to have some complaints voiced online from angry customers.

- **Be wary of merchants who approach you unsolicited**. It is best to not open and delete e-mails you receive from businesses that you do not already have some form of a business relationship with. An example of this might be an e-mail from a person claiming to be nobility in a foreign country who needs to sell jewelry, a yacht, or other high-priced item at a ridiculously low price because of civil unrest or something similar. These are almost always scams and should be avoided.

- **Save records of the transaction after you have made the purchase**. The online merchant will present a receipt page and prompt you to print a copy of the receipt for your records. If you do not have access to a printer, you should at least make note of the transaction number because you may need this information to contact the merchant about the item you purchased.

- **Stay on top of the account you use for online transactions**. You should make sure that the total amount of the purchase matches the amount debited from your account. Also, look for any unauthorized charges.

Most credit cards companies offer protection to consumers when making purchases online. For example, Visa offers a zero liability policy that reimburses charges made to credit cards fraudulently. MasterCard SecureCode allows cardholders to create additional passwords that will be required before online purchases will be authorized. Discover will provide temporary, valid account numbers that can be used in lieu of the actual number imprinted on the credit card. American Express monitors purchases and contacts cardholders if a questionable transaction occurs. To find out which specific online purchase protection your credit card company offers, visit the official website.

Here is a list of some of the websites for credit card companies:

- Visa (**www.visa.com**)
- MasterCard (**www.mastercard.com**)
- Discover (**www.discovercard.com**)
- American Express (**www.americanexpress.com**)

PayPal

PayPal allows users to transfer money from your account to anyone who has an e-mail address or mobile phone number. Keep in mind that the recipient must have a PayPal account in order to obtain the money if he or she does not yet have one, but this process is free.

Use PayPal to pay for purchases on eBay, send money as a gift, or receive payment for services rendered. Many merchants offer discounts to customers who pay for online purchases using a direct debit from a PayPal account. Additionally, PayPal account holders can obtain debit cards that are linked to their PayPal accounts.

There are fees associated with some PayPal transactions. If you receive PayPal payments as a form of payment for services rendered, keep track of the total amount of PayPal fees you pay for these transactions because you may be able to claim this amount on your taxes as a business expense. Talk to a tax adviser regarding this type of deduction.

A PayPal account is also essential if you intend on selling items through online auction websites. You can use the account to receive payments and track your income. As a buyer through auction websites, using PayPal as a form of payment will allow you to buy items from sellers who only accept this form of payment.

PayPal is not the only way to send money online, but it is one of the most popular and widely used websites for this purpose. If you already have a PayPal account you should check to make sure that you are using it to the fullest advantage, and if you do not yet have a PayPal account you may want to open an account. PayPal is not the only company offering this type of service. For example, Moneybookers.com and Alertpay.com both offer similar services. Make sure that whichever service you choose is conducive to your needs.

You do not need a PayPal account, or any other type of online money transfer service for that matter, unless you are specifically required to have one to accept payments by an employer or for some other reason. On the other hand, already having an active PayPal account can save time if you want to make an online money transaction. If you choose to open a PayPal account, visit the website (**www.paypal.com**) and click on the "sign up" link. You will be asked to decide which type of account you want to open — personal or business — and will then have to provide your personal contact information including your full name, mailing address, e-mail address, and telephone number. You will also be asked to provide a credit card number or bank account number as a back-up funding option, but this is optional.

A business account is an appropriate choice if you do business online, such as selling merchandise or providing freelance online services. Choose a personal account if you simply want to be able to send money to friends and family and use the PayPal payment features on merchant websites.

CHAPTER 8

ONLINE INVESTING

This chapter is for any type of investor — whether you have invested in the past or not. You will benefit from this information even if you have never invested a penny. This is a great time to get involved with investing, specifically because of the accessibility to online investment information and easy access to opening and maintaining investment accounts online. No longer is investing a mysterious activity left to people with financial degrees. Anyone with Internet access and a few dollars to spare can become an investor without ever having stepped foot into a professional investment adviser's office.

Keep in mind that this does not mean you should arbitrarily pick investments without any rhyme or reason. You want to make sure you understand where you are investing your money and that you have the ability to monitor your online investment accounts. The good news is that researching various investments has never been easier because just about everything you need to know is online. Find reliable online sources for investment information and only use money that you can spare to lose, and chances are, you will have a successful investment future ahead of you.

CASE STUDY: FINDING MORTGAGE HELP ONLINE
Managing Investments Online

After I became interested in investing, it was just a natural gravitation to invest online. I already banked with USAA and found it convenient to set up a separate brokerage account through them.

I use USAA for my online trades and MSN Money for cursory research. I utilize ValueLine for third-party research. I use Mergent Online for financial statements and StockScreen123 for screening, which is a filter that helps you pick stocks based on what you are looking for. The best part about using the Internet for investing is the convenience. It is simple to track your investments and take inventory of your positions. Buying and selling is merely one or two clicks and net gains/losses are automatically recorded.

For me, I use the Internet as a means to execute investment decisions. I think it is absolutely necessary to use the Internet to gather research. However, if I have any criticisms about using the Internet for investing, it is the plethora of information you are constantly given.

Every investing website will provide stock price updates by the second, and this promotes a level of activity that is unwarranted for me and other long-term investors. I still find myself being unduly influenced by what the Internet feeds me versus my own reason and understanding.

If you have not yet tried investing online, remember that using the Internet for investing is akin to using the Internet for banking. You may be naturally hesitant at first, but once you have done it, you will wonder how you ever went without it.

Before Investing

Most financial experts agree that one of the most important steps you can take before getting involved with investing — online or otherwise — is to first make sure that the rest of your finances are in order. If you have followed the advice of this book thus far, you have already taken some important steps to getting your finances in great shape:

- You manage your financial accounts online and pay close attention to how your money is being spent.

- You have a budget in place and utilize online tools to help you stay within your budget and track your spending.

- You know how to access the Internet safely and how to spot an Internet scam.

- You know how to use the Internet to help you save money, which helps your overall financial situation.

Are your finances in order? A good way to tell if you are ready to start investing is to ask yourself whether you have money you would not lose sleep over if it were beyond your control or gone altogether. Why should you only invest money you can afford to spare? Investing always involves a certain degree of risk. For this reason, you should not invest money that you need for things like your mortgage payment or the week's groceries. Relying on investment income to pay bills or other necessary expenses can be a very bad idea, especially for people who have little money to invest in the first place or are new to investing.

For this reason, do not feel like you absolutely have to invest just because the Internet makes it so easy to do so. Investing can be a great way to make money (and a good way to lose money), but if your personal finances are not in order, gaining control of your money should be the priority above investing. It can be difficult to resist the urge to hop into the realm of online investing feet first, especially considering there are so many advertisements reminding you how easy it is to open an account.

If your finances are in order, but you have not yet started investing, now is the time to start. If you are a seasoned investor, but have never tried to manage your investments online, you will find the transition easy and rewarding.

Start Investing Online

If you have never invested before or your investment experience has not amounted to more than signing up for an automatic monthly withdrawal from your checking account to an investment account, then this section will help you determine where to invest, how to invest, and how to manage your investments.

If you are unsure of the investing process, try using an investment simulator to see how the money you invest might potentially grow or shrink. Investopedia.com features an investment simulator that is free and allows you to use a simulated $100,000 and see what the money would do based on the investments you would make. Always remember that these simulators are not guarantees of how your own investments will pan out, but are a good way to get the feel for what investments might do. In other words, if you become an instant millionaire with your simulator, the same thing might not happen for you when real money is invested.

Here are some other investment simulators to consider:

- Wall Street Survivor (**www.wallstreetsurvivor.com**)

- Investopedia (**http://simulator.investopedia.com**)

- Fidelity (**www.fidelity.com**)

Opening an account

The actual process of opening an investment account online varies depending on which website you choose, but generally, you can expect to provide personal contact information such as your full name, address, telephone number, and e-mail address. You will also be asked to provide identifying information including your social security number and the social security number of the person you designate as your account beneficiary in the event of your death.

You might also be asked about your employment status and need to provide employment information. You might also have to provide copies of your driver's license or some other identification to prove you are indeed who you claim to be.

When filling out the form, make sure you provide accurate information. If you have any questions during the process, use the assistance provided online by the website or call the customer service telephone number. Some online investment websites, such as Scottrade (**www.scottrade.com**), have local offices with representatives who can also assist with registering online and opening an account.

Step 1: How much can you invest?

An important question to consider when preparing to invest is how much money you can afford to invest. Luckily, investing does not require a huge initial monetary contribution, nor do you have to provide a significant amount of money each month in order to maintain your standing as an investor. This is one of the advantages of investing; even a small amount of money invested on a regular basis can eventually grow to an impressive sum.

So how much money can you afford to invest? Look to your budget for the answer. If you are utilizing online tools such as Mint.com, you may already have a good idea of how much money you can afford to invest because the online tool will tell you. You can also look at it this way: After you have paid all the bills, contributed to your savings account, and set aside money for fun extras, how much money is left over? If the answer is "Not a lot," you might want to start cutting expenses in order to do some investing, but do not cut corners so much that you cannot manage to cover your monthly expenses.

If the rate of return you can potentially earn from investing is lower than the interest rate you currently pay on your credit card and loan debt, you may want to aggressively pay down the debt balances before putting money toward investments. You should only invest money that you can afford to lose, and if you have massive debt, you likely do not have money to spare. Do not drop down to making minimum debt payments because you want to have extra money to invest. In most cases, this does not make any financial sense at all. You will invest money and receive a return, but in reality, you will save more money by paying down the high interest debt.

Step 2: Why do you want to invest?

The amount of money you invest, as well as the investments you make, should be dictated by your financial goals. For example, if your goal is to save for retirement, you should put your money into long-term investments that feature a low level of risk. You will probably also want to diversify your investments so all of your money is not invested into one specific type of investment. You do not want to put all of your money into a single type of investment, because if that investment does not perform well, all of the money your have invested will perform poorly. On the other hand, if your goal is to earn as much money as possible in a relatively short period of time, you will probably wind up putting your money into some riskier investments that have a higher rate of immediate return. With the goal of quicker returns, you may focus more on specific investments instead of diversifying your investment portfolio, as your goal is to make money as quickly as possible and you are willing to accept the risk associated with a portfolio that is not diversified.

If you are not sure of your financial goals for investing, have a look at where you stand now. Do you already save a sufficient amount of money for retirement, or can investing be a great way to augment your existing retirement savings? Are you simply looking for the thrill and excitement that can come with investing because the rest of your finances are in order? Determining how investing can help you now or in the future is important, because it can help you decide which type of investing you should start with.

Step 3: Start small

Investing can be intriguing and even a little fun, but it is always important to remember that you are dealing with actual money and it is not a game. You should also realize that you will probably be bombarded with information and options that might try to steer you into complicated and risky investments, but in the very beginning, it is better to start small and then delve into more complicated investment endeavors after you are more experienced.

Find brokerage that offers services online that will not only allow you to invest, but will also guide you through the process and help you determine how much you can invest and where you should put your money. A great starter website for new investors is E*TRADE. This website is designed for new investors who are not sure of the first steps to take and might be a little apprehensive about the whole process. E*TRADE offers the following features and options:

- The website features online databases of information to answer most investment questions.

- You can open an investment account on E*TRADE and manage the account with the help of the E*TRADE professionals or automated guidance tools.

- E*TRADE will analyze your current financial standing and provide suggestions as to which investments you should make and for how much money.

- As you maintain your account, E*TRADE will allow you to make changes to your investments and will continue to provide guidance.

E*TRADE is not the only website that is appropriate for beginning investors. ShareBuilder.com, Scottrade.com, and Schwab.com can assist beginning investors with learning about the investing process as well as how to properly maintain investment accounts for maximum return potential. Most online brokerages offer similar services and initial set-up procedures; although, they might vary slightly from one to another. No matter which website you choose, look through the website before investing to make sure you understand how much you will pay in fees for each trade or for the maintenance of the investment account. You will also want to know the rules and regulations regarding Internet transactions. What happens if you submit a request for a trade that is not done because the website experiences an outage? Can you reach a customer service representative immediately by phone if you have questions, or is it difficult to discern how to contact the company? Can you cancel a transaction request after it has been submitted?

These are the types of questions that you will want to know the answer to before signing up for an account with an online investing website.

Maintaining Your Online Investment Account

Seasoned investors might not need a review of conducting trades and maintaining an investment account. If you are new to the world of investing online, however, it is a good idea to learn more about what you can expect to encounter. After you have opened your online investment account, you will need to maintain the account and make some financial decisions, such as when to increase the amount of money you invest or when to sell some of your investments. You will be better prepared to do so if you already understand some of the concepts involved.

LEARN THE LINGO

Stock certificates: Documents that prove ownership of a stock.

Street name: Shares held in the name of the brokerage instead of the name of the individual buyer.

Direct purchase: Buying stock directly from the company instead of through a broker.

Limit orders: The minimum or maximum price you set for buying or selling stock.

Forex: The Foreign Exchange Market, where foreign currency is bought and sold.

Diversify: Having a variety of investments instead of only one or two.

Making the Trade

Online trading takes place at the speed of light. No paper changes hands; no one shouts "Buy! Sell!"; no certificates are bundled and mailed by a clerk on a bicycle. Billions of dollars flash around the world every second, 24 hours a day, seven days a week. In the time it took you to read this paragraph, untold sums were bought and sold. Somewhere in this mix of digitized cash, your order for 100 shares was placed and fulfilled.

When you open your online trading account, you will be asked to provide information about yourself and the type of account you wish to hold. You might be asked to set up a money market fund, which is a deposit account designed to hold the funds you will use for online trading. You will be asked to deposit money into the online account to open your trading account. You will be told how to access your statements and asked whether you would like paper copies mailed to you and, if so, how often. Other information may be asked for or offered.

Your online broker will offer a trading page. It will ask for the name of the company or fund whose shares you wish to purchase or the company's stock symbol. Ford, for instance, uses "F" as its trading symbol.

Keep in mind that the price of financial instruments is constantly changing. The number of "buy" orders versus the number of "sell" orders will determine whether the price of the stock is going up or down. You may see a company's stock at $25 and submit a buy order for 100 shares, but actually pay something more or less than $25, reflecting the market change in the seconds or minutes between your decision and the fulfillment of your order.

When you click "buy" or "sell," your order is sent to a huge database of transactions. The database will search for the lowest or highest price, depending on whether you are buying or selling. The database matches buyers and sellers together and fulfills the orders, sending confirmations to both ends. The order is then registered and an electronic record of the transaction is recorded. There is a three-day period, which is termed Settling Trades in Three Days and abbreviated to T+3, in which you must provide payment for your transaction.

Limit orders set the price at which you will buy or sell a stock, meaning you set the amount of money you wish to buy and sell stock for. For example, suppose you place a limit order with your broker or the website, giving instructions to buy stock in a certain company at $50. Right now, the price is at $55, but you think it will drop, and then go back up. The purchase will not be made until the stock hits $50, because this is the limit order you set in advance.

Other terms you should understand and discuss with your financial adviser include:

- **Cash account:** A standard brokerage arrangement in which you, the investor, put a specific amount of money into an account and use that cash to purchase investment instruments.

- **Selling short:** A strategy that attempts to make money when the price of a stock goes down. In essence, you place a bet. Typically, you "borrow" the shares of the company in question and sell them immediately, pocketing the cash. At some point, you buy back the same number of shares and return them to wherever you borrowed them. The gamble is whether the price will have dropped or risen in the interim. If it drops, as you guessed, you make a profit. If it climbs, you lose money. For instance, if you sell the borrowed shares for $50 and later buy them back for $25, you have made a tidy profit. If the shares jump to $75, you take the loss. Short selling is not for novice investors.

- **Going long:** The opposite of short selling. Going long involves purchasing stock expecting that it will go up in price over time and you will sell it for more than you paid for it.

- **Buying on margin:** A strategy that allows you to borrow money to purchase stocks. You must set up a margin account with your broker and comply with the rules governing such accounts by maintaining a specified percentage of your purchase in your account. You must pay interest on the amount borrowed and, of course, repay the money, so your exposure can be significant if the stock you purchase goes down and you lose money. Margin accounts are not advisable for amateurs. You should become a seasoned online investing long before you start making investments using credit.

- **Options:** Allow you to buy or sell an instrument at a specific price within a set period of time. Suppose you purchase options. If your option is to buy, it is known as a "call." A call allows you the right to purchase a given stock for a set amount of money at a later date. You pay for the right to purchase the stock at a certain price, and if you fail to actually make the purchase at that price, you lose the fee. If your option is to sell, it is known as a "put" and is the reverse of the call. In the hands of knowledgeable, market savvy people, calls and puts can produce huge profits. In the hands of inexperienced investors, calls and puts can produce huge losses.

Options themselves are traded and investors can purchase calls or sell them and buy puts or sell them. Nothing is free and brokers have options' fees and/or commissions that you should know about before you attempt to play the market at this level. You can research these fees by visiting the websites for brokerages or by speaking to individual brokers, but you can generally expect to pay a fee of $5 or more.

This means your actual, realized profit margin on your portfolio is being eroded by fees, costs, interest, and other expenses, all of which go to someone else, not you. This is another reason to know the cost of your investment decisions. It is human nature to be optimistic about our decisions, and investment choices are no different. Many people, especially new investors, believe the sun will always shine, and the price of their stock will always go up. Eventually though, a rainy day comes along, and prices go down.

Stock funds, which are mutual funds managed by financial professionals, are the easiest way to get into the market because you are putting your money into the hands of professional managers who know all of the ins and outs of the markets. By doing basic online research, you will be able to see which funds have had the best performance over the past one, five, or ten years. Do not be dazzled by recent success of any given fund. Rather, look to past performance as well as current management.

Individual stocks, which are purchased on an individual basis instead of in a mutual fund, are riskier for new investors who may not have the market sophistication to properly research companies and then the market instincts to either sell or buy at appropriate times. It is best to begin modestly, with a few stocks, to get a feel for the market and then expand your investments as you gain experience both with the markets and with your online broker.

The following is a drill that might help you learn how the markets perform and how good you are at picking stocks. Before you put any money into a portfolio, chose several stocks you might be interested in buying and track them for a week or so. Are they performing as you expect? What is the market saying about these companies? How are they doing against their competitors? Check their prices daily, and try to learn why their prices rise or fall. Do they react to economic news? Sales figures? International events? This way, you can test your instincts without putting any money into play. You might also want to try one of the simulated trading programs mentioned earlier. These programs will allow you to simulate investing in certain stocks and estimate how your investments will perform, so this can be a good primer before investing actual money.

Investment quiz

What type of investor should you be? Take this quick quiz and find out. Answer True or False to each of the following questions.

1. You like to have a firm grasp on how your money is being spent, and it makes you nervous to allow someone else to handle your finances for you.

2. People who do not check in on their investments daily might miss something.

3. You love researching investment information and reading financial commentary.

4. There is plenty of money to be made by investing, and you know you are the type of person who will earn a great deal of money through your investments.

5. You have ready access throughout the day to the Internet.

If the majority of these statements elicited a response of True from you, there is a very good chance that you are an active investor. This means that you not only want to personally manage your investments on a certain level, but you are also willing to do the research yourself to determine how your investment dollars should be spent. If most of your responses to the quiz were False, this points to a passive investor. This means that you have the money to invest, but would rather have someone else manage the investment decisions for you. You probably will not actively review your account, and in fact, many passive investors set up automatic withdrawals from their checking accounts into their investment accounts and never really think about the money they are putting into their investments at all. They know they have investments and might glance at the statements they receive periodically, but for the most part, they are not active participants with their investments.

Passive investors need to make sure that they have competent advisers managing their investments. They should also take the time to review the statements they receive because they should be aware of whether they are making or losing money. Being a passive investor is not necessarily a bad thing as long as you are willing to put in a little effort and not ignore your investments altogether.

Ideally, there is a happy medium between a very active investor and a very passive investor. You should be willing to accept some risk, yet not be so risky with your investments that you do not care if you lose money. The Internet can help you research investments and manage your investment accounts, but you should not be absolutely consumed by your investments. Use the Internet to your advantage to manage your investments, but do not use it so extensively that you wind up overwhelmed with the constant desire to monitor your accounts.

CASE STUDY: EXCERPT FROM THE COMPLETE GUIDE TO ONLINE INVESTING: EVERY-THING YOU NEED TO KNOW EXPLAINED SIMPLY

By Michelle Hooper

Many investors have the knowledge they already need to make investments, but there are times when you are just not sure what to do and when to do it. This is where investment brokers come in. Stock markets can crash one day and be right back where they were the next day. There is no trickery involved here, it is just the way the markets work, and there is nothing anyone can do about it.

Investors must be educated and resourceful when making investments; although, many seem to follow the trends, which is not always the best thing to do. Investors get scared and pull out of stocks when they drop, frightened they will lose all their money. In some respects, this is a good decision — unless that stock skyrockets the next day.

There are beginning investors and mainstream investors. Beginners should start out small and work to develop an investment portfolio that brings desirable returns while seeing excellent cash flows. The cash flow is the progress of a stock company where the actual cash that flows through is measured during a specific period. In reviewing a company's income statement, depreciations are deducted in addition to other expenses, resulting in determining the net income of a company. Beforehand though, that total number is the actual cash flow. Rate of return is what you expect from your investment before taxes. Mainstream investors are the higher-net individuals who are not afraid to lose $20,000 or so. Really though, no one wants to lose anything.

Investing is easy, but it is not meant for everyone. If you get mad at casinos, then you should probably hire a broker. Stock markets offer a variety of sources, such as the National Association of Securities Dealers Automated and Quotations, the American Stock Exchange, Dow Jones, and more, each of which is updated regularly as the times and the numbers change frequently. No doubt, the market is a whirlwind of information; you have plenty to learn.

Seasoned Investors

If you already have an investment account, or several investment accounts, find out if it is possible to access and manage these accounts online. Your investment company likely offers online access and has probably been courting you to manage your account online through e-mails and brochures in your monthly statements. If you are happy with the service you already receive from your current investment company, and the fees associated with online investing fit your budget, then signing up for online access to your investment accounts is a great idea. There is an excellent chance that your brokerage offers online access; visit the website to find out or speak to your broker.

Are you nervous about the prospect of moving the management of your investment accounts online? If your investments have always been solely handled by your broker, or if you still get nervous about managing your checking account online, try to think of the positive aspects to online investment management. You will have instant access to your investment accounts. You will never have to wonder how your investments are performing, and you will never have to wait on hold over the phone to speak to a representative to find out the balance of your account or how a fund is performing. If you are nervous about accessing investment information online, take it slowly and step by step. Start by reviewing your accounts online. Once you have had a chance to utilize this technology, you will likely soon grow comfortable with the idea of conducting investment transactions online. You might even become comfortable with reviewing your investment accounts on your Blackberry while waiting for a table at a restaurant. Instant access to your investment accounts — and all of your other financial accounts — is not something to feel anxiety about, but instead should be regarded as a way to get a firmer grip on your finances.

If your investment brokerage does not offer online access, or if you are not impressed with the online access offered, you have a wide variety of options available to you. Do keep in mind that if any of your investments fall under the category of retirement funds, you need to switch the company you use to manage these funds in a specific way. You cannot merely close the account and receive a check, because this will be considered an early withdrawal and will be subject to penalties and taxes. Talk to your tax adviser or a representative from the new company you intend to use to find out about properly rolling the retirement investment funds into a new account.

Choose your online investment company carefully if you do decide to switch. As a seasoned investor, you already know which features will be most useful to you and what you are willing to spend for trades and other services. Some websites allow you to be quite passive with your investments while others are designed specifically for investors who want to take a hands-on approach. If you are involved with complex investments, such as Forex or other fast-moving investments, you should look for a website that is specific to these transactions, which will allow you more options.

A word of caution: If you have been a relatively passive investor because you did not have online access to your investment accounts, take care not to go overboard with managing your account once you do sign up for online account management. It can be enticing to have online access to transfer funds or make additional investments at any time of the day or night, and some investors spend much more time worrying over their investment accounts than they should. Though it is certainly true that you want to manage your investment account appropriately, and you should always be aware of how your investments are performing, remember that some investments that are specifically designed for long-term growth have the best potential to earn money when they are left alone and allowed to grow. If you are constantly logged on to your investment account online, fiddling with your funds, and moving money around, you may be doing more harm than good.

Consider signing up for notifications that will inform you when something happens with your investment accounts that you might want to investigate. For example, if you invest in individual stock, you may be able to sign up for an automatic notification that notifies you when your stock falls to a certain range. Most websites will not only send you e-mail notifications, but you might also be able to register for text message notifications over your cell phone as well. This might be a good way to keep track of the things that would otherwise keep you awake at night, because you would feel compelled to constantly check your account online.

Treat your online investment accounts just as you would any other financial account that you access online. Take care when accessing your account using a computer that is not your own, and do not share your username and password with anyone else. Additionally, if someone claiming to be a representative from your investment company contacts you through any means and asks questions about your account number, do not reveal any information that might give an identity thief access to your investment account. Contact your investment company to find out if it was a valid attempt to contact you, and if not, report the attempt so your investment company can take appropriate action.

The Top 10 Online Investment Mistakes

Investing online is not a seamless process. Avoid the following mistakes that are made by both seasoned and new investors alike:

1. **Not researching fees.** You may pay fees for trades, withdrawals, or opening an investment account. Though some investment websites pride themselves on having as few fees as possible, others will charge a fee whenever possible. There is definitely a difference between the various investment websites. Take the time to find the company that suits your needs without piling on the fees.

2. **Not researching investments.** It is not necessary to have a finance degree to know that certain investments do not make much sense. The Internet is simply too full of great information for you not to learn something about where you should be putting your money.

3. **Being too aggressive or too passive.** You should become familiar with your investment goals before you start investing. If you are investing for the long term, do not put all your money into volatile, short-term investments. If your plan is to invest short-term, do not choose an investment that grows slowly.

4. **Forgetting the money you invest is actually money.** The virtual environment of the Internet can sometimes make investments seem abstract. Some investors get so carried away with the thrill of moving their investment dollars around that they lose perspective and do not act as cautiously as they should.

5. **Ignoring your money.** It is one thing to be a relatively passive investor, but it is another entirely to be a completely absent investor. If you have no interest whatsoever in managing your investments, it is incredibly important for you to find an adviser or automated program that will do it for you. Try to talk yourself into at least reviewing the statements you receive from your investment company so you can see how your investments are performing.

6. **Getting carried away.** If you find yourself checking your investments on your Blackberry while you are in the middle of a conversation with a friend or coworker, there is a very good chance that you are getting carried away with online investing. It is great to have constant access to your investments, but it should not absolutely consume you.

7. **Complicating your money.** If you are a new investor, stick with beginning investment programs, like mutual funds until you feel comfortable moving on to more advanced investment options, such as short sells. You should not begin your online investment experience in a get-rich-quick scheme. Instead, look for solid investments designed for first time investors.

8. **Panicking.** If your investments are in the stock market, it is important to remember that stocks go up and down, and this pattern re-

peats often. This is why beginning investors are urged to not invest money they cannot afford to lose; if the money you have invested will not necessarily be missed, you are less likely to panic the second a stock drops a little.

9. **Only investing.** Investments are supposed to augment your savings, not replace them. Even though your online investment accounts seem very similar to your online checking and savings accounts, they are very different indeed. Your savings accounts accrue interest no matter what, but the performance of your investments is not guaranteed. Do not fool yourself into thinking that you do not need to put money into your savings account as a result of having a robust investment account.

10. **Sticking with one investment.** You may start with one certain type of investment, but as you mature as an investor, you should start to diversify your investment accounts. The Internet can be an invaluable tool in this situation, because you can research what investment products are appropriate for you in your effort to diversify.

Online investors make other mistakes too. For example, with so many investment experts posting information online, it is too easy for everyday people to begin to feel well-versed in investment topics as a result of reading what the experts write. Although it is true that you should follow your instincts when it comes to online investing, your instincts should also be tempered with good research from a variety of sources. There is not one person who knows everything about investing online, regardless of what degrees or practical experience an expert touts. Take advantage of information offered by more than one expert, and make sure the expert is actually an expert before putting too much trust into what the person says. For example, an article from The Wall Street Journal is probably a more credible source than a blog written by a college student who has a passing interest in investing. Also remember that advice from credible sources can sometimes be skewed depending on who is paying the expert to say what he or she is saying. A financial expert might appear on a website ad making the proclamation that now is the time to invest in gold, but if the financial expert is employed by a company that sells gold as investments, the expert advice is biased.

CHAPTER 9

MANAGING LONG-TERM SAVINGS

Sometimes, money barely spends a moment in a checking account before it is sent right back out to pay bills, make purchases, or be put to some other use. This is relatively normal for checking accounts because they are designed to be fluid accounts with money filtering in and out constantly. You already know how to manage your checking account online, but what about those accounts where money sits for a very long time such as retirement accounts or college saving accounts

You may not have even thought about accessing accounts that you do not actively use on a daily basis over the Internet. The truth is that there is great benefit to having online access to these accounts, even if you do not put much thought into them. Even if the account is designed to build interest for a very long period of time, it is still your money.

CASE STUDY: THE ONLINE
ACCESS ADVANTAGE

Ben, touring musician

In a world of super-fast technology, it is a total security blanket to know that you can access your bank account instantly online. As a person who works in the entertainment industry, it is often hard to visit a bank branch with my horrendous schedule. With my bank in particular as well as many others, getting a checking account balance and history is merely just a text message away. Within seconds of a transaction, you can see your spending activity and trends. I can also do fund transfers right from my phone. It is amazing. Many people frown on the fact that accessibility is too easy, and many people are scared of the proverbial "hacker," but to be honest, so many security measures have been put into place to ensure your safety.

I think online banking is the greatest invention since currency!

Your Retirement Accounts

If you do not have any retirement savings at all, now is the time to get started. You have the advantage of all the information available on the Internet to help you determine which retirement account is suitable for you. Additionally, you can use the Internet to open the retirement account, set up automatic withdrawals to the retirement account from your checking account, and manage the account to ensure that you are saving as much money as you need to in order to live comfortably throughout retirement.

How are you supposed to know how much money you need to save monthly in order to sufficiently fund your retirement? The answer depends on several factors:

1. How many years do you have until you retire?

2. How much money do you already have set aside for retirement, if any?

3. What do you anticipate your debt to be upon retirement? For example, will you have a monthly mortgage payment, or will your home be paid off?

4. Do you plan on working part-time in your retirement?

5. Will you have other sources of income, such as social security or a pension?

6. What standard of living do you want to have in retirement?

7. Will you be asked to financially assist adult children while in retirement?

Obviously, there are many factors to look at when determining how much money to save for retirement. If you are starting your retirement savings early in your adulthood, then you have a distinct advantage over people who are already nearing retirement age because compound interest will help your money grow exponentially. If you are older, yet have not started saving for retirement at all, keep in mind that it is certainly better to start late than to not start at all. The Internet can help you determine how much money you should save — by using online retirement calculators — and what type of retirement fund to have — by researching credible sources online for tips and advice.

What qualifies as a retirement account? Retirement savings are designed specifically for use after the account holder reaches a certain age and come with potential tax advantages. Withdrawals from these accounts before retirement are usually taxed substantially with very few exceptions, in addition to fees and penalties assessed by the financial institution holding the account. When looking for a retirement account, make sure the account is specifically designed for retirement savings and for long term growth.

No matter where you decide to put your retirement savings, online access is a definite feature you want to have. Even if you will not check in on these funds on a regular basis because your retirement is not in the near future, it is important to be able to review your retirement accounts instantaneously when you do want to have a look.

If you already have retirement accounts, check with the financial institution to find out what you need to do in order to gain access to the accounts online. If the financial institution that holds your retirement accounts is the same financial institution that holds your checking account or some other account, you may already have access to your retirement account and just never realized it. Try logging on to your account to see whether you can indeed access your retirement savings the same way you access your other accounts held with the financial institution. Most online accounts will list every account you hold with the financial institution when you first log on. For example, if you have a checking account and a credit card with your bank, then you may be able to view both of these — or at least the account numbers linking to more detailed information — when you log on to the website. Look for your retirement savings accounts here, and if you cannot find the information either on the main menu or by doing some searching, contact a representative to find out how to gain access.

If you cannot gain access to your retirement savings through the same website that you access your other accounts, it might be that you have to register for access using a different process or your retirement savings might be managed through a different provider with a different website.

When you sign up for account access, you will be asked to go through a similar — if not identical — process that you went through when initially signing up for online access to your regular checking account. You will probably be asked to create a username and password. Use the same caution that you used when creating your login information for your other accounts, and ensure that the information cannot be easily guessed by other people. Be sure to also bookmark the website where you sign in for account access so you do not have trouble finding it again the next time you want to view your account activity.

If you do not yet have accounts set up specifically for your retirement savings, you will find that the Internet can help you determine the best retirement accounts as well as how much money you should put away every month. Use a website such as Vanguard (**www.vanguard.com**) or Fidelity Investments (**www.fidelity.com**) to start researching retirement accounts available to you and to help you calculate how much money you should plan to deposit into your account every month. Websites such as Bankrate. com (**www.bankrate.com**) also offer a wide range of retirement advice and calculators, but will not try to sell you specific retirement account products because they are not directly affiliated with one retirement account provider.

LEARN THE LINGO

Compound interest: Earning interest on interest that has already been earned.

Maintaining retirement accounts

The amount of time you spend maintaining and reviewing your retirement accounts mainly depends on what type of accounts they are. For example, you might spend more time reviewing a retirement account that is tied directly to investments than you would spend maintaining a retirement account that is a simple deposit account because investments can fluctuate and you might need to change the funds you have invested in if they do not perform well. The more action required to maintain your retirement account in an effective way, the more time you can expect to spend online. The good news is that it is usually far easier to maintain your retirement account online than it would be to maintain the account through the postal mail or by visiting a local branch of the financial institution holding the account. For example, if you want to make a change to your retirement account, you might be able to make the change online in seconds instead of sending this request via postal mail.

College Savings Accounts

College savings accounts are intended to help pay for college and are commonly opened by parents or other family members long before their children head to college. Savings accounts that are specifically designed for college costs are similar to retirement accounts in that they might have tax advantages for people who qualify based on income and can last for a very long time. Some parents open college saving accounts for their children right after birth, hoping to take advantage of the benefits of compound interest over the years. If you do not have a savings accounts for your child's college education, you may wonder whether it is too late to start or whether it will be a waste of money if you are not entirely sure whether your child will eventually attend college. Use the Internet to help you determine how to save for your child's education — no matter when you start saving —

and find a flexible account that will suit the needs of your child. Online calculators can help you determine how much money you need to save monthly in order to afford college tuition and other college costs by the time your child is ready to head off to college.

You may be pleasantly surprised to find that there are a wide variety of savings products designed specifically to help parents save for their children's college education, all of which are detailed in great length online. Use the Internet to help you decide which college savings account is most appropriate for your child by reading about the pros and cons of each. Do you want an account that is transferable to a sibling in case one child decides against college? Do you want to pre-purchase college tuition in a certain state? Do you want an account that you can open on behalf of your grandchildren? Whatever your situation, there is an appropriate college savings account available including 529 plans and Coverdell Education Savings Account (ESA), which is also referred to as an education IRA. The offerings vary from state to state, and some college savings accounts only provide tax benefits for people who fall within a certain income range. A great website to review for more information regarding college savings is Saving For College (**www.savingforcollege.com**).

Find out which college savings accounts are available by visiting your existing financial institution's website. Review which college savings accounts are offered and then research what other financial institutions are offering. It is also a great idea to use an online search engine such as Google or Bing to search for tuition pre-purchase plans specific to your state.

Bankrate.com offers an excellent source online for parents to learn more about finding the right type of college savings accounts: Savingforcollege. com. This helpful website compares the various college savings accounts available in each state. There are also college cost estimators available that can help you determine how much money you should save each month based on the type of college your child wants to eventually attend and how many years you have left before your child is college-bound. This is not the only website offering this information online, but it is one of the best and easiest to use.

Once you have college savings accounts in place, you may not have to monitor them for growth on a very aggressive basis. While you do want to know how much money you have in the account and how much interest you have earned, a parent of a five-year-old child probably has no reason to check the child's college savings accounts on a daily basis. Do make sure that you sign up for online access to the college savings accounts and enroll in electronic statements so you do not have hundreds of paper statements that need to be filed. It is a good idea to make a conscious effort to review these accounts on a regular basis, such as quarterly when your statements arrive in your e-mail inbox, but do not feel obligated to check in on the accounts every single day because with long-term savings, it may be nothing more than a big waste of your time. You should simply take the time to occasionally make sure that everything within the accounts is correct and the balance is growing as expected.

What if you never manage to save a dime for your child's college education? In this instance, you can use the Internet to help your child apply for Federal Student Aid, find scholarships, or apply for student loans. All of this information is available at the Federal Student Aid website (**www.fafsa. ed.gov**). Or, if all else fails, help your child scour the Internet in search of a part-time job that will help pay for his or her college education by using a job search website.

enefits at once, but instead, it might grant you access to multiple
view information about your benefits.

online access to benefits is outsourced to a separate company
necessarily a direct subsidiary of the company you work, and
any might handle the human resource functions for your com-
ployees.

not sure if you have online access to your employee benefits,
human resource (HR) representative with your place of employ-
find out. An HR person within your company should be able to
u to all of the online resources you need as well as provide you
special account information you might need in order to access
sites. Some websites require initial login using information specific
mpany you work for, but then every time you log on thereafter,
uld be able to use the username and password you create in order
your information.

vork for a small business, there may be no HR person to guide you
the process. You might need to ask the business owner to show
w to get access to your benefit information online. Regardless of
in charge of helping employees access benefit information using the
t, someone should be able to assist you. If you do not know who it
your supervisor.

companies provide this information to employees using an intranet
rather than the Internet. An intranet system allows you to access
formation from your work computer using Web pages that are not
ible outside of the company's network. If this is the case, you should
he same precautions when accessing your information through the
any's intranet that you would when accessing your information on

CASE STUDY: A SEASONED INTERNET USER

Carol, working mother

I have used Internet banking since the early 1990s, which is before many people started using the Internet for this purpose. The main reason I use online banking is because I save so much time paying my bills, and I also love the convenience of the process. I save money paying bills online too because I do not have to order paper checks nearly as often, not to mention to money I save on the cost of envelopes and stamps. The convenience is the best part. I have the ability to receive a bill in the mail one day and then turn around and pay it online with the due date in the future and forget about it. I really like how my bank gives me the option of setting payments up as much as 30 days in advance. This is incredibly convenient because I never miss a payment.

Additional savings are gained because my bank does not charge me any fees for paying my bills online. Saving money while conveniently paying my bills online is fantastic.

CHAPTER

MANAGING
YOUR BENEFI

If your employer provides you with additional benef
check, there is a good chance that they might also pr
to manage your benefits online. Online self-service o
which allows employees to manage their benefits onli
ing directly to a human resources representative, save
because there are fewer questions to answer and less
with. If the company you work for offers online access
sure to sign up so you can have access to your benefits
The process of signing up varies depending on the sys
uses, but it generally involves accessing a personalized w
ing a password and logon provided by the company for
Your employer might not provide one website that enabl

of your be
websites to

Often, th
that is no
this comp
pany's em

If you ar
speak to
ment to
direct yo
with any
the webs
to the c
you sho
to acces

If you v
through
you ho
who is
Intern
is, ask

Some
system
the in
access
take t
comp

your home computer using the Internet. Do not share your logon information with anyone else, make sure other employees are not watching over your shoulder while you access your benefits information, and be sure to log off the system completely when you are finished so that no one can sit at your desk after you have left and see everything you accessed. Keep your accounts for your employer-provided benefits secure — just like you would for your checking account or credit card account.

LEARN THE LINGO

Intranet: A computer network that is only accessible by authorized users and is not accessible without a password.

Copayment: Money that you will be expected to pay out of pocket for medical services.

Medicare: A federal program providing medical coverage to senior citizens.

Health Care Coverage

Do you know which medical procedures are covered through the health insurance your employer provides you? Do you know how much money you will have to pay out of your own pocket when you go in for an eye exam? If you need to see a psychotherapist, are you sure that your insurance company will accept the claim sent in for payment by the psychotherapist's office? There is a very good chance that you can find out all of this information — and much more — on your health insurance company's website.

Your health insurance company's website will usually allow you to look at specific coverage, submit a claim, check on the status of a claim, and speak one-on-one with a customer service representative using a chat function. If you have ever called an insurance company and been put on hold just to ask a simple question about coverage or to check on the status of a claim, you can certainly appreciate the ability to log on to a website and find all of the information you need.

Why is it important to know what type of medical coverage you have? Knowing what your personal financial liability for medical care will be is an important part of overall personal financial management. If you already know that your copayment for a routine medical office visit will be $30, you can have the $30 ready before walking into the doctor's office. If you know that your medical insurance will not cover a certain procedure, you can find an alternative way to pay for the procedure, or you can elect to not have the procedure at all if it is not required to keep you healthy. You should know exactly what you can expect your health insurance company to pay for and what you should expect to pay for so there are no financial surprises that you are unprepared for.

Signing up for online access for your health insurance usually involves visiting the website for the insurance company and creating a username. The initial password for access to the website might be provided to you by your employer. Speak to a representative of your employer to find out how to access to your health insurance benefits online.

Depending on the type of medical insurance you have, and the procedures in place by the health insurance company, your financial obligation and rules for submitting claims will vary. This is why it is important to understand the particulars of your policy; do not assume that just because your friend was able to get a certain medical procedure completely covered by the company, you can get the same procedure with no out of pocket expenses too. There are simply too many variables from one policy and insurance company to another for you to make assumptions about your coverage without verifying the information first.

Retirement Funds

You already know about using the Internet to manage the retirement funds that you open and maintain yourself, but what about the retirement funds that are offered through your employer? Many companies offer retirement funds in the form of 401(k)s, Thrift Savings Plans (often referred to as TSPs), annuities, and pensions. The good news is that some employers will match a portion of your financial contribution to these tax deferred retirement accounts, making the accounts all the more lucrative and helping you better prepare for your financial future.

If you do not currently participate in a retirement program, which might be partially funded by your employer, and you know that your employer offers these benefits to employees, find out whether you are eligible to enroll. There may be "open seasons," also referred to as open enrollment periods, offered by your employer, which are periods of time throughout the year when employees can enroll in the retirement program or make changes to existing accounts. Once you know whether you are eligible to open a retirement account through your employer, conduct some research online to find out whether it is in your best interest to enroll with your employer or whether your money will be better off in a different type of retirement account.

Use the Internet to research the retirement account options offered by your employer. If you know the name of the company that handles the retirement funds, visit the official website of that company and read about the performance of the funds. The process of signing up for online access to your retirement account varies from one employer to another. Speak to a representative or follow the online tutorial (if available) to access your account.

How do you know whether you are already saving enough for retirement without the help of your employer? Use an online retirement calculator to determine how you might benefit from additional retirement savings. Though it may seem like putting more money toward retirement is always the best option — especially when some of the money is practically free, as it might be provided by your employer — you should take a look at your personal finances as a whole. If you are knee-deep in debt, now may not be the time to add another retirement account to your portfolio. If you are convinced that a retirement account through your employer is a far better option for you over the retirement funds you already have in place, use the Internet to research the proper steps to discontinue funding one retirement account and funding a new one.

IRS rules regarding retirement accounts provided through your employer can be confusing, but using the Internet to find the answers to your questions can save you a lot of time and effort. Be sure to confirm any information you find that does not come directly from the website for the retirement fund or a credible source within your company. You do not want to make assumptions about moving money to an employer-provided retirement account without ensuring that moving the money will not result in hefty penalties.

Your Paycheck

Chances are good that you do not actually receive a paper check from your employer, but instead, you might receive your paycheck in the form of direct deposit to your bank account. Although direct deposit is a great way to receive your money and can certainly streamline your personal finances, sometimes employees do not bother to view the information that used to come with paper pay statements such as deductions and vacation hours accrued. These statements are usually still issued by employers, either in paper or electronic form, but because the pay statements is not attached to a paycheck, some people simply do not bother to read the statement at all.

If your employer offers access to your pay statement online, take advantage of this option. Make a point of accessing your pay statement online every time you receive your pay through direct deposit. What should you look for on the pay statement? You should verify the following information:

- Is the amount of money listed on the pay statement the actual amount that was deposited into your account?

- How many vacation days have you accrued?

- Do your taxes look correct? Might it be time to reevaluate the number of tax exemptions you list?

- Are the number of hours worked listed on your paycheck accurate?

- Is all your contact information up to date?

A problem with your pay statement should be caught early and brought to the attention of your employer. This is especially important during the first few months of employment or when the payroll procedures change. Make sure that everything on your pay statement is accurate so there are no problems receiving your money.

If you want to determine how making changes to your tax exemptions might affect your paycheck, or if you wonder whether an increase to your retirement account would make your paycheck too small to cover your monthly bills, use a paycheck estimator, such as the one available at Pay-checkCity.com, to play with the figures and see what changes you can make to your paycheck without changing the amount of money you receive each pay period too drastically.

Pay statements that are made available to employees through an Internet or intranet site are not difficult to review. It usually involves logging on to the site and viewing the statement using Adobe Reader or other computer software. Make it a habit to utilize the online access offered by your employer and quickly review your statements each time you are paid. This feature will also come in handy if you need to quickly print a copy of your pay statement to accompany a loan application or for other purposes.

If your employer does not offer the option of viewing benefit information online, approach your employer about reconsidering. There can be financial advantages to offering these documents online including savings gained by not printing and sending documents, and self-service options may result in fewer employee questions directed toward the human resource department.

Some employers simply do not offer online access because they do not think that it is a need or want of the employees. Make your request known and assure your employer that online access to benefit information will simplify and enhance the total benefit package.

Social Security

This particular benefit does not necessarily fall into the category of benefits provided by your employer. Social security is a benefit nonetheless, and it is something that you can learn a lot about online. Learn about the benefits that you will receive upon retiring or that your dependents might receive upon your death by searching the Social Security Administration's website (**www.ssa.gov**).

The system behind qualifying for social security payments — and eventually receiving these payments — can seem mysterious and a little bit confusing for people who are not familiar with the system. Many people are only vaguely aware that regular paycheck deductions include social security, and some people have absolutely no idea how much money they can expect to receive from this program when they reach retirement age. The program is demystified by accessing the official Social Security Administration's website.

Documents necessary for requesting a social security card, your statement of social security earnings, and an estimation of your eventual social security payments are all available on this website. Knowing how much money you can expect to receive on a monthly basis from social security can help you when you are planning your retirement savings or when you are nearing retirement and want to know what your monthly budget is going to look like.

If you are already retired and already receive social security benefits, you can use the website to apply for Medicare or to switch the financial institution where your social security funds are direct deposited. Depending on your nearest SSA location and turnaround time when visiting the office, these tasks might have taken an entire afternoon to accomplish if you had visited a physical social security location. Using the Internet, these tasks are completed in a few clicks.

People nearing retirement age should take the time to review the social security website. You can learn everything you need to know about your eventual benefits. Having this knowledge before entering retirement can help you make the decisions relating to when you should retire and how much money you should budget for living expenses after you stop working.

CHAPTER 11

MANAGING
TAXES ONLINE

How many times have you wondered about a tax-related issue, yet did not research the answer because you figured that it would take far too long to track down a reliable answer to your question? Taxes can be complicated, even for people who do not itemize deductions or have any dependents. How do you know what income to report to the Internal Revenue Service (IRS)? Should you record tips you receive? Can you get a tax break for going to graduate school? What if you cannot afford to pay your taxes and need an extension? These questions, and other tax-related questions, can be answered online quickly and without waiting in line for hours at a local IRS office or seeking the advice of an expensive accountant.

The Internet can be a great tool to help you manage your taxes, but first, it is important to remember a few things about managing taxes online:

1. **Just because the information is online does not mean it is true**. Choose credible sources for your tax information. For example, a forum on an unofficial tax website or a blog post from someone who is not a tax professional should not be considered credible sources.

2. **The information may apply to some people but not others.** Not all tax deductions apply to all people. Annual income, family size, and geographic location are just a few of the factors that can change the tax rules for people. Be sure to research information specific to your situation.

3. **Not knowing a tax rule is not grounds for not paying**. Ignorance is certainly not bliss when it comes to taxes. Use the Internet to find out what taxes you owe, if any, and how to go about paying the taxes in a timely manner and maybe even reduce your tax obligation for the next year.

4. **Seek out professional help when needed**. You can find a great deal of reliable tax information online, but there are some questions that have so many gray aspects to them that it is simply best to seek out professional advice. In this instance, use the Internet to find a Certified Public Accountant (CPA) or to contact an IRS representative to get your tax questions answered.

Online Resources

For a government entity that is often ridiculed for having such complicated jargon and regulations, the IRS offers a refreshingly easy website to navigate. Using the IRS website (**www.irs.gov**), you can find out any tax information you need.

What information can you find on the IRS website? You may be impressed by the answer. Almost any tax question you have can be answered by visiting the IRS website. If you cannot find the answer to your tax question by clicking on the subject links provided, use the search engine on the website to search for your answer.

Obtain any IRS forms and publications directly through the IRS website. You can also file your tax return on this website, check on the status of your tax return, and read about the latest tax legislation that may affect the amount of money you owe or receive as a refund when you file your taxes. For example, if you think you may be eligible for a new tax credit, but you are not entirely sure if you qualify, you can find the answer using the IRS website.

If you cannot find the answer to your tax question on this website, use the "Contact Us" function on the bottom of the Web page to find out how to get your question answered. You may be directed to contact your local IRS office or to e-mail a specific department to get your issue resolved.

Please note: IRS.com is not the same thing as IRS.gov. IRS.com is a website run by Banks.com and is not affiliated with the IRS at all. Although you can get information from this website that may help you, it is important to realize that this website is not the official website for the IRS. If you are looking specifically for the IRS website, be sure the Web address you type is **www.IRS.gov**, not www.IRS.com.

Non-IRS sources

What if you need tax recommendations? Sometimes, a different perspective can help you make a decision regarding your taxes. If you find the wording on the IRS website confusing, you may be able to find the same information using language that is easier to understand from a different online source. Just remember that if the tax information does not come from the official IRS website, then it may not be legitimate. In other words, if you wind up audited by the IRS, you cannot cite information you received from Banks.com or Bankrate.com as justification for making a tax mistake. The information provided by websites such as these is for informational purposes only and should never be considered a substitute for information directly from the IRS or from a tax professional such as a CPA.

In fact, most credible tax information websites will give you great information, but will then urge you to verify it with the IRS or your tax adviser, as tax regulations can change and each person's tax situation is different. You cannot hold these websites liable for giving you information about taxes that is not accurate or does not pertain to you. For example, some tax information only pertains to people within certain tax brackets. It is up to you to make sure that the information correlates with the information on the IRS website.

Visit websites such as the aforementioned Banks.com or Bankrate.com to find tax advice. These sites provide both business and personal tax information. Other great resources include SmartMoney (**www.smartmoney.com**) or H&R Block (**http://hrblock.com**). If you have questions pertaining to your state taxes, go to the official website for your state and search for tax information.

The tax alarmists

If you search online for tax information, you will inevitably find a website that makes the claim that taxes are unconstitutional, illegal, or downright evil. You will also find websites that claim there are easy steps you can take to no longer owe taxes at all, and if you order a book or pay a membership fee to the website, you will learn the easy steps and be free from your tax burden forever. *Take the information featured on these types of websites skep-*

tically. The information you read on these websites is often alarmist and, at times, downright ridiculous. At first when perusing these websites, you may chuckle at some of the wording or roll your eyes at the claims made, but if you research information on multiple websites with this type of information, you might start to wonder whether there may be something to what these folks are saying after all.

When in doubt, contact the IRS or a tax professional. It is highly unlikely that you will stumble upon a hidden secret online that allows you to stop paying taxes and not wind up in jail. Use the Internet to help you find a way to lessen your tax burden, not to figure out a way to stop owing taxes altogether.

Estimating Taxes Online

Suppose you have already researched everything you want to know about your taxes. You now understand why you owe taxes, you know the deadline for filing your taxes, and you have started saving receipts so you can get as many deductions as possible when tax time rolls around next year. Your next question will probably be something along the lines of "How much will I actually owe?"

For some people, the question is not about how much they will owe, but rather how much they can expect to receive as a refund. Either way, you can use the Internet to estimate what your tax obligations will be so you can start planning for the tax bill — or planning for what you will do with your refund. Use a tax calculator offered by TurboTax (**www.turbotax. com**) or the IRS website.

Just as with loan payment calculators discussed in Chapter 7, you need to keep in mind that any figure you receive from using an online tax estimating tool is only an estimate and might not be exactly the same amount that your taxes turn out to be. There are simply too many variables to consider for a simple online calculator to give you a figure that is 100 percent accurate. Consider the number you receive to be an estimate.

The IRS website features a calculator that can help you decide whether you need to change your withholding on your paycheck. If you are looking for information regarding how much money you will owe, you can find a simple tax estimation calculator on the H&R Block website (www.hrblock. com). There are plenty of other websites offering this type of tax estimation tool, so if you do not like the one offered through H&R Block, research the Internet and find one to your liking or visit one of the websites listed in the Appendix of this book.

Tax software

Tax software, such as TurboTax, can be purchased in stores or online and will help you determine how much you owe or will receive as a refund. Choose tax software that has online capability. You want to be able to use your tax software to not only help you figure out which deductions you can take and how much you will owe, but also to submit your taxes electronically via the Internet.

TurboTax is one of the most popular tax software programs available. Use the software on the TurboTax website (**http://turbotax.intuit.com**) to help estimate your tax obligation or refund and then file your taxes electronically. Other websites offering similar features include TaxAct (**www. taxactonline.com**) and CompleteTax (**www.completetax.com**).

If you file Form 1040EZ, which is the form designed for filers without itemized deductions, and your taxes are relatively straightforward, there is really no reason why you should have to visit, and pay, a tax preparer to file your taxes for you. You can file your taxes online, in some instance free of charge, and have your refund — if you are due a refund — much faster than you would have if you had mailed your tax return into the IRS.

Filing income taxes online is not only for people with simple taxes. You can still prepare and file your taxes online despite having multiple deductions or running a home business. To figure out which tax software program is best for your needs, visit a software comparison website such as Tax-Compare (**www.tax-compare.com**). This website will show the features of the highest rated tax software programs and will provide links to the website for whichever tax preparation software you choose. Keep in mind that the cost of tax preparation and filing might differ depending upon your tax situation. If you have a simple tax return, electronic filing might be free, but if your taxes include several different forms, your cost will go up exponentially.

Look for a software program that comes with a guarantee. Because the software is taking the place of a tax adviser, most of the software companies provide a guarantee that any errors or omissions from your tax return that are the fault of the software program will be covered by the guarantee. This means that a software glitch is not going to wind up costing you thousands of dollars in taxes and penalties. Refer to the software information to find out how to file a claim against the guarantee. On the other hand, if the software does not come with this type of guarantee, the company has no liability relating to mistakes on your taxes.

CHAPTER 12

PERSONAL PROPERTY MANAGEMENT

When you think about your personal finances, you probably think about the money you have sitting in your bank account or maybe even the debt you have piled up on your credit card. Do not forget to include your assets while getting your personal finances in order — and not just the monetary assets you have sitting in a financial institution. Your personal property — your car, your household belongings, your jewelry — are all part of your financial picture as a whole. You can use some of the tools offered online to help you manage these important assets.

Home Inventory

A home inventory is a detailed listing of the personal belongings within your home. If your home were to burn down in a fire while you are out of town on vacation, how difficult would it be for you to supply your insurance company with a complete list of your belongings including the estimated values? If you have a current home inventory, it would probably not be a huge ordeal, but if you have never taken the time to conduct a thorough home inventory, the task of making your insurance claim would be quite difficult. You may wind up getting less money than you are entitled to simply because you cannot remember everything that went up in flames.

Conducting a home inventory is actually not very difficult with the help of tools found online including forms and instructions for creating a home inventory. You can compose a home inventory on your own with paper and a pen, but using the Internet to assist you with creating the list can be much easier. Find suitable home inventory forms for each room in your home by conducting an online search using your preferred search engine and use these as guides for conducting your home inventory. You should then store your detailed home inventory on your computer and a location that is separate from your home, such as a safety deposit box or at a relative's house. This will ensure that you can still access your complete home inventory even if everything in your home — including your home computer — is demolished. You also have the option of saving your files off-site using a service such as Barracuda Networks (**www.barracudanetworks.com**). In the very least, send a copy of your home inventory to an e-mail address that you can access from any computer, such as Gmail or Hotmail.

You should conduct a home inventory whether you are a home owner or a renter, regardless of whether you have a home full of stuff or a tiny apartment with only the bare essentials. A home inventory will be of great assistance should you need to file an insurance claim.

How to home inventory

If you are willing to spend money for the creation and maintenance of your home inventory, consider using a service such as the one offered through

Home Ownersite (**http://home.ownersite.com**). This website will allow you to create a complete home inventory using the template provided. You will also have the option to upload photographs of your belongings and store them along with the home inventory on the website's database. There is a charge for this service, but if your main concern is a simple process and reliable online storage of your home inventory, the cost may be worth it to you.

LEARN THE LINGO

Home inventory: A list of the belongings within your home.

Template: A document or graph that has already been created but leaves open spaces for personalization.

Insurance riders: Additional insurance purchased above the standard policy.

Term life insurance: An insurance policy set for a specific number of years with a monthly premium that does not change.

Tax deduction: A reduction in your tax obligation.

Withholdings: Deductions that are taken from your paycheck to pay taxes and other obligations.

Market value: The amount of money an item will reasonably sell for.

Equity loan: A loan secured by the equity in your home, also referred to as a second mortgage.

If you are looking for a free way to inventory the contents of your home with the help of the Internet, find a website offering free home inventory forms. Many insurance websites, such as State Farm, offer free printable home inventory forms, and there are also many websites dedicated specifically to providing free forms. These are not difficult to track down online and are often quite easy to use. Home inventory sheets that are room-by-room can make the task less daunting and can also compel you to be more detailed about your personal property within your home.

Home inventory sheets should give you the opportunity to write down what the personal property item is, a physical description of the item, the estimated value of the item, and any additional notes you may have. Make note of serial numbers for electronics and take pictures of any valuable items such as art or jewelry.

Update your home inventories as you add or subtract from your personal belongings. It may seem like an arduous task right now, but in the event of a large-scale insurance claim, you will be really glad that you took the time to conduct a home inventory and kept it updated.

The following sample home inventory form will give you an idea for one way of formatting your sheet.

ITEM	DESCRIPTION	ESTIMATED VALUE	ADDITIONAL NOTES
Couch	Blue sectional	$650	In good condition
Table lamp	Rooster design	$80	
Rug	Blue and white design, tassel edges	$1200	Purchased in Turkey, certificate of authenticity in safe
Side table	Dark wood, oval shape	$140	Long scratch on top
Recliner	Blue, over-stuffed	$300	

Insurance

Your insurance is designed to protect your belongings and finances. Your car insurance and homeowner's or renter's insurance protect you in the event of damage to your car or domicile. Life insurance protects the financial needs of your loved ones in the event of your death. There are other types of insurance available to protect just about anything you can think of, from insurance to cover your jet skis to insurance specifically designed to cover medical costs if you get cancer.

What do you need to know about insurance and the Internet? You should know that you can conduct a wide variety of insurance tasks online, including:

- Obtaining quotes from a variety of insurance companies to find out which policy is the best price

- Comparing coverage options to determine whether additional insurance riders are a good idea or a waste of your money

- Maintaining your coverage once it is in place, making payments, and adjusting coverage options

- Making claims online and monitoring the status of those claims

- Finding answers to your questions in the FAQ section or by conducting an online chat with a representative

If you are shopping around for an insurance policy, you will quickly find that the Internet is an invaluable tool.

Car insurance

If you have car insurance already in place, get access to your policy online. This will allow you to see how much money you owe for your next premium, exactly what type of coverage you have, how much your deductible is, and how much it will cost to alter your coverage. You will be able to print proof of insurance directly from your own computer and estimate how much your insurance premium will be if you purchase a different car.

As with access to other online accounts, you will probably have to create a username and password in order to access your information. Once you have done so, be sure to also sign up for electronic notifications so you will stop receiving your insurance statement in the mail every month. While you are logged in, you will also be able to set up recurring monthly payments that will automatically be deducted from your checking account if you have not already done so. All these steps will save you time in the end and will make it much easier to keep your insurance policy in order.

Homeowner's or renter's insurance

It is important to keep an eye on the insurance policy that protects your home and the belongings contained within your home. Things change, and one major purchase can suddenly make your policy insufficient for your needs. You need to make sure that you are always covered for the full value of the repair or replacement of your home and your belongings.

Additionally, one of the benefits of this type of insurance is the liability coverage that accompanies the rest of the coverage. If someone visiting your home slips, falls, and ends up in the hospital with a broken arm, you might be sued for the cost of the medical bills, as well as other expenses your guest incurs as a result of the injury. If you are found liable as the property owner, the costs associated with a lawsuit can be staggering. Homeowner's insurance protects you from these exorbitant costs.

Obviously, these are policies that you do not want to accidentally let lapse. Some types of insurance coverage, such as flood insurance, will incur a 30-day waiting period before you will be allowed to renew if you accidentally allow the policy to lapse. Additionally, a lapsed homeowner's insurance policy may be in violation of your original agreement with your mortgage lender. This is where having online access to these insurance policies is so important; you do not want to miss a single payment or accidentally allow the coverage to lapse. Accessing the policy online will allow you to verify that the policy premiums have been paid, which can be of special concern if your homeowner's insurance is paid by your mortgage service as a portion of your escrow account.

If you do not yet have online access to your homeowner's or renter's insurance, visit your insurance company's website to find out how you can gain access.

Life insurance

Depending on which type of life insurance you have, you may not find yourself checking in on your policy online very often. Some life insurance policies, such as term life policies, will not change from month to month so there is really no reason to spend much time monitoring the particulars of the policy.

Nonetheless, online access is a great idea. If you have a question about your policy, or if you would like to change the terms of the policy, online access might allow you to conduct your business online without ever having to speak to a customer service representative.

Use the Internet to research your options when deciding which type of life insurance policy you should obtain and when trying to figure out how much money the policy should be worth. You can also use the Internet to find life insurance if you have difficulty finding a company to issue you a policy, either because of your age, a preexisting medical condition or some other factor.

Market Values

How much is your stuff worth? There are a few different reasons for knowing the value of your belongings, including:

- You may be asked to state your net worth on a loan application, and knowing the value of your assets will make this estimation easier.

- If you decide to sell your property, you want to know what a fair asking price will be.

- Knowing the market value of your belongings will help you understand your overall financial situation better. For example, if you realize you owe more on something than it is worth, you can then decide what your next course of action should be.

Using the Internet to find out the value of your car or home is incredibly easy. In fact, in most instances, it is absolutely free.

How much is your car worth?

You will want to know how much your car is worth in several instances, such as when deciding whether you can afford to drop some of your insurance coverage. You can also find out the estimated value for a car that you are thinking about buying, which will help you in the negotiating process when you actually go to buy the car.

Although there are many sources available online to find out the estimated value of a car, one of the best is Kelly Blue Book (www.kbb.com). You may already be familiar with Kelly Blue Book; many people looked up the value of their vehicles in the printed books this company issues before the advent of the Internet. Though the books are still available in some forms, most people turn to the Internet version that is available free of charge.

To find out the estimated value of a vehicle you will need to know the year, make, and model of the car. It also helps to know which options, such as leather seats and tinted windows, are installed on the vehicle as well as the estimated mileage. You will also be asked about the general condition of the car. All of these factors are taken into consideration and the website returns with a few different values: the private resale value, the amount of money you can expect to pay a dealership for the car, and how much money you can expect to receive as a trade-in when buying another car.

How much is your home worth?

Your home may not be worth what you think it is worth. You need to know the market value of your home if you are planning on refinancing, obtaining an equity loan, or preparing to sell your home. Putting your home on the market for far more than it is actually worth can prove problematic for the eventual sale of your home.

The market value of the home is not necessarily how much you owe on the mortgage, nor is it worth exactly what you paid plus whatever improvements you made. Home values are more complicated than that and are influenced by the values of the homes surrounding your home as well as any recent home sales in your area. Always check the market value of your home before putting it up for sale and look at the market value — not just the asking price — for a home before you submit a bid to buy the property. Remember that just because a home is listed for sale at a certain price, does not necessarily mean that the price is what the home is worth. Avoid a situation where you pay too much for a home by first checking the market value.

or false. The Internet can be an amazing tool for getting to the bottom of things, especially after you have accumulated some experience visiting various websites and learning how to search effectively to find the information you need.

Financial news

Staying on top of financial news used to involve awaiting the newspaper every morning and then pouring over the money articles to find out what the economy was doing. It is far easier to obtain financial news using the Internet, and there is no need to wait for a daily newspaper.

Subscribe to a financial news source online by finding a news source you trust and then clicking on the "subscribe" link. You may have to pay for full access to some of the well-known publications such as *The Wall Street Journal* (**www.wsj.com**) or *Kiplinger* (**www.kiplinger.com**), but the cost of subscribing to the online versions of these publications are usually lower than having the publications delivered to your home.

If you have Internet access on your mobile phone, you can access financial news wherever you are. Some cell phones offer applications that allow users to peruse current financial news, or use the Internet function on your cell phone to visit your favorite financial websites. Downtime spent waiting in line or awaiting the start of a business meeting can become productive time to catch up on financial news.

Subscribing

If you come across a particular finance website that you like, you can usually subscribe to an e-mail feed, which will result in articles appearing on the website being automatically sent to your e-mail as they are published. You decide which ones you want to read and delete the rest. This can be a great way to subscribe to the writings of a certain columnist or blogger who you find informative or entertaining.

To subscribe, look for a link on the website that says "RSS Feed" or "Sign up to receive articles directly sent to your e-mail." Keep in mind that signing up may also entail agreeing to receive advertisements and other unsolicited e-mails.

CASE STUDY: ONLINE RESEARCH
Kari, stay-at-home mom

Over the past few months my husband and I have been looking forward to opening a college fund for our daughter and finally opening a retirement account for us.

For some of us, most of the information that people throw at you is confusing or just goes right over your head; I am a part of this group. The researcher in me, however, will not give up; hence my love of the Internet. For a few days, I began looking up different types of college funds. To my surprise, I actually found it somewhat easy to distinguish the differences between the various college savings accounts available. Not only was I able to decide upon what type of account to open, I actually found which bank we would like to open it up through.

While looking for college funds, I also began researching individual retirement accounts (IRAs). I will admit it was a little confusing at first, but after a while (and with my husband's help), we decided what path we would take. Overall, the Internet was an invaluable resource in deciding which accounts to open.

Financial forums

If you like to chat with other people about personal finances, or if you like to see what other people are chatting about in relation to how they spend and save their money, join a forum or two. These online conversations featured on websites are ongoing and usually contain an interesting mix of people, some of whom are seasoned financial experts and others who are completely baffled by all topics pertaining to money. You can learn plenty from participating in forums, and you may actually make some online friends too.

To get started with a forum, you might have to first register as a user and await permission from the Web master to join the forum. Once you have access, you simply sign into the forum and either add to an existing conversation — called a "thread" — or start a new one.

The following are a few important things to remember when participating in forums:

1. You can never be sure that the person writing a post in a forum is actually who they say they are.

2. You will usually have to register with a website before you can participate in forum discussions. You can choose your own settings that hide your real identity and deny access to your e-mail address if you would like to.

3. General Internet etiquette calls for respectful conversations on forums. It is okay to disagree with another forum poster, but calling the person an idiot might get you thrown out of the forum.

4. You should never lend money to someone you meet in a forum, nor should you get involved with a business venture with a person you only know through an online forum.

Forums can be particularly useful for people who are trying to change their financial behaviors and would like some encouragement from other people. For example, people with shopping addictions, gambling addictions, or who are recovering from bankruptcies can all find support from online forums set up to help these specific groups.

The following is a brief list of some financial forums available online:

- **Wise Bread (www.wisebread.com)**: A forum devoted to living well with a limited budget.

- **The Clark Howard Show (http://clarkhoward.com)**: Forum topics range from finding discounts on retail items to retirement fund advice.

- **myFICO (www.myfico.com)**: The forum on this website is dedicated to credit score topics.

Use common sense when participating in forums online. You can have fun and learn many different things from the other members of the forum, but do not consider the information you receive from random forum posters to be completely accurate.

The best sources

Where do you go when you have a question that you cannot trust to anyone but the experts? There are some websites that are far more accurate and reliable than others.

Your financial rights

If you want to learn more about your rights as a consumer regarding banking, credit, and all other money matters, visit the official website for the Federal Trade Commission (FTC) (**www.ftc.gov**). The FTC is in charge of protecting consumers and enforcing the laws that are in place to assist people with their personal finances.

If you want to know more about identity theft, stopping unsolicited credit card offers, or how to deal with a collection agency, the FTC website should be the first place you visit online. Follow the links provided on the website to file a complaint or contact an FTC representative.

State-specific money laws

Anything that is specific to your state should be featured on the website your state presents. For example, if you want to know what the statute of limitations on credit card debt, it is best to visit your state's website, because these laws vary from one state to another. Similarly, bankruptcy laws can be different among states, so trusting broad bankruptcy advice you find online can prove problematic. Search for your state's website using a search engine.

Commercial sources

Simply put, some financial websites are better than others. There are some personal finance websites that consistently present timely and accurate information without charging visitors to access the information.

Bankrate.com is one of the best personal finance websites for general financial information, ranging from savings to debt. If you are looking for information regarding saving money as a consumer, Clark Howard's website (**http://clarkhoward.com**) provides a wealth of valuable information.

Clark Howard is a consumer advocate and television/radio host who hosts shows about saving money and avoiding financial scams.

If you are looking for information specific to an account you have, the financial institution that holds the account is always the best source. Find the website address of your financial institution by looking at your account statement, contacting a customer service representative, or using a search engine.

See the Appendix of this book for a listing of valuable websites that will help you with your personal finances. Most of the websites listed in the Appendix were mentioned within the text of this book and will give you further information that will assist you in creating a budget, getting technical help with your computer, and more.

CONCLUSION

YOUR FINANCES
WILL THANK YOU

The Internet is one of the most valuable tools at your disposal. Not only do you have a vast library of financial advice from experts and lay people alike, but you can also use the Internet to get your complete personal financial picture into perspective. Managing your money may have been a time-consuming project that you avoided in the past, but once you turn to the Internet for help managing your money, things become simpler.

Even if you have never been an organized person, or if you have never done a very good job of managing your money, online resources and tools can transform your financial situation into a highly effective, highly organized, well-oiled machine.

If you have always managed your money effectively, yet have never taken the steps toward using the Internet to help you with your finances, there is an excellent chance that you will be amazed at how much more time you have on your hands once you no longer need to spend hours at your desk reconciling your bank statement or researching investment funds. Allow the Internet to work for you, and you will be pleasantly surprised at what it can do.

Be ready to evolve as the Internet evolves. Times change, and so does the Internet, so do not cling to only one way of conducting your personal transactions online. Embrace new technology, look for new financial management tools available online, and do not be afraid to try new things.

You have all the tools at your disposal to take charge of your money and make it work for you, and now, you have a thorough knowledge about how to get started. Keep this book as a reference for when you need a little help with navigating your transition to effectively managing your personal finances online. It will not be long before you are surfing the Internet like a champ and managing your money online as if you had never done it any other way.

APPENDIX

LIST OF HELPFUL WEBSITES

Budget Assistance Websites

Mint.com (www.mint.com): A free site that allows users to manage their money and does the bookkeeping for the user.

Spending Diary (www.spendingdiary.com): Offers a simple way for users to track their spending.

BudgetTracker, Inc. (http://budgettracker.com): Allows users to track their transactions instantly on the Internet or through a phone. Users can save all their transactions into a calendar.

Financial Software Websites

TopTen Reviews (www.personal-finance-software-review.toptenreviews.com): Offers reviews of top personal financing software.

Personal Finance Informational Websites

Bankrate.com (www.bankrate.com/): The Web's leading compiler of financial information.

Kiplinger (www.kiplinger.com): Based in Washington, D.C., this is a publisher of business forecasts and personal finance advice.

The Clark Howard Show (http://clarkhoward.com): A radio show that advises consumers how to protect their savings.

CreditCards.com (www.creditcards.com): Provides users with information about credit cards in different categories, such as low-interest cards and rewards programs.

FindABetterBank (www.findabetterbank.com): Helps users find a bank to suit their needs and provides information to banks on why users are switching to or away from them.

Tax Websites

Internal Revenue Service (www.irs.gov): The website of the Internal Revenue Service.

Federal Trade Commission (www.ftc.gov): The website of the Federal Trade Commission.

TurboTax (http://turbotax.intuit.com): Guides users through filing their taxes step-by-step and double-checks to make sure all the information is filed correctly.

H&R Block (www.hrblock.com): The world's largest tax preparation business.

Consumer Advocate Websites

Better Business Bureau (www.bbb.org): The Better Business Bureau strives to be the leader in building trust in the marketplace.

Coupon Websites

These are online sites where users can find coupons to be used at various outlets.

RetailMeNot (www.retailmenot.com)

CouponCabin (www.couponcabin.com)

CouponHeaven.com (www.couponheaven.com)

DealCatcher (www.dealcatcher.com)

Value Estimate Websites

Kelley Blue Book (www.kbb.com): Provides a database in which users can find pricing information on any vehicle.

Zillow (www.zillow.com): Provides a database of real estate pricing for users.

Merchandise Websites

eBay (www.ebay.com): An online auctioning site where users can buy and sell anything in auction format.

Craigslist (www.craigslist.org): A site where users can post anything they wish to sell, arranged by location of where the sale is taking place.

Internet Safety Websites

Barracuda Networks (www.barracudanetworks.com): Provides various products aimed to deliver security solutions to computer users.

McAfee (www.mcafee.com/us): Provides security solutions for computer users, such as antivirus software.

Investment Websites

E*TRADE (https://us.etrade.com/e/t/home): Online investing site that is easy-to-use for people new to investing and also provides 24/7 service.

Government Websites

Social Security (www.ssa.gov): The website of the U.S. Social Security Administration.

FAFSA (www.fafsa.ed.gov): The federal website of Federal Student Aid, an office of the U.S. Department of Education, which provides monetary assistance for students to go to college.

Money Transfer Websites

PayPal (www.paypal.com): A site that allows users to make secure payments online.

Social Lending Websites

Virgin Money (www.virginmoneyus.com): A branch of Virgin, which also offers music and mobile phones, that is designed to make personal financing easy for users to understand.

Prosper (www.prosper.com): Pioneered peer-to-peer lending, which allows people to invest in each other. Also offers an auction format for lending.

Lending Club (www.lendingclub.com/home.action): A financial community for creditworthy investors and borrowers to find each other for loans.

BIBLIOGRAPHY

Brad Hill. *Getting Started in Online Personal Finance*. Wiley Publishing, 2000.

Matt Krantz. *Investing Online for Dummies*. Wiley Publishing, 2007.

2009 Identity Fraud Survey Report. Retrieved 1 July 2010 from *<https://www.javelinstrategy.com/research/brochures/brochure-128>*

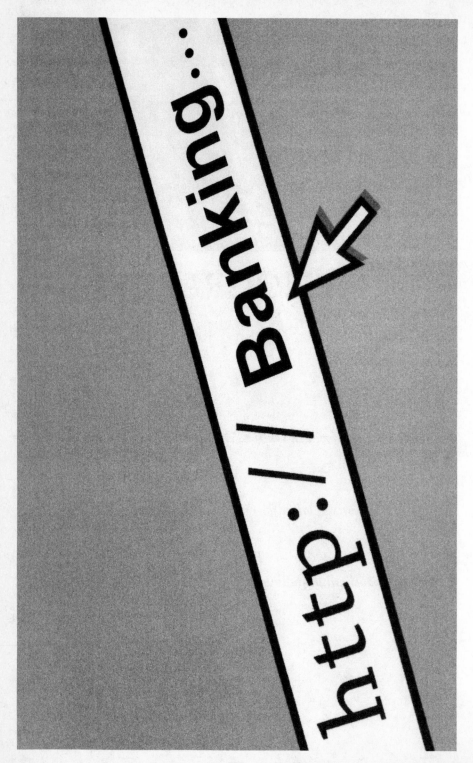

AUTHOR BIOGRAPHY

Tamsen Butler is the author of *The Complete Guide to Personal Finance: For Teenagers and College Students*. She is also the personal finance blogger for Banks.com as well as the featured expert for LoveToKnow.com's *Ask the Mortgage Expert*. She has also written for TheBudgetFashionista.com as well as other fun financial sites. She has two vibrant children and stays busy with graduate school, writing, and volunteer work.

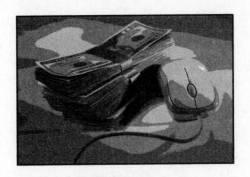

INDEX

1040EZ form, 246

A

Alertpay.com, 195

Amazon.com, 42, 186

American Express, 194

AnnualCreditReport.com, 160, 217, 276

Apple iPhone, 34

B

Bankrate, 272, 244, 267, 87, 138, 149, 154, 162, 177, 180-181, 225, 227

Bankrate, 272, 244, 267, 87, 138, 149, 154, 162, 177, 180-181, 225, 227

Bankrate, 272, 244, 267, 87, 138, 149, 154, 162, 177, 180-181, 225, 227

BANKS.com, 162, 177, 243-244, 281

BarracudaNetworks.com, 250, 274

Big E-Z Books, 45

Bing, 48, 83, 227

Blackberry, 214, 217

Bookmark, 49, 84, 225

Brute force attack, 53

Budget Stretcher, 143

BudgetSimple, 142, 145

BudgetTracker, 143, 146, 271

Buying on margin, 208

C

CardRatings.com, 162

Chase, 130, 163

Checks Unlimited, 122

Cisco, 62

Clark Howard, 266-268, 272

CNNMoney, 154

CompleteTax.com, 246

Consumer Credit Counseling Service, 133

CouponCabin.com, 185, 273

CouponHeaven.com, 185, 273

Craigslist, 191, 274

CreditCards.com, 87, 162, 272

CreditCards.com, 87, 162, 272

D

Dave Ramsey, 144, 148

DealCatcher.com, 185, 273

Dell, 73, 277

Deluxe, 43, 122

Dictionary attack, 53

Direct deposit, 48, 80, 105, 115, 236-237, 238-241

Direct deposit, 48, 80, 105, 115, 236-237, 238-241

Disk Cleanup utility, 65

Disk Defragmentation utility, 65-66

D-Link, 62

Dow Jones, 212-213

E

eBay, 42, 190-191, 195, 274

Equifax, 158, 160, 218, 276

Escrow.com, 192

E-statements, 98-100, 102

Experian, 158, 160, 218, 276

External hard drive, 71

F

FAQ, 48, 81, 88, 94, 167-168, 253

Federal Student Aid, 228, 275

Federal Trade Commission, 107, 218, 267, 273

Fidelity, 201, 225

FindABetterBank, 87, 272

Flash drive, 71-72

Ford, 206

Forex, 205, 214

G

GasBuddy.com, 184

Gateway, 73, 277

Going long, 208

Google, 39, 48, 83, 98, 227

Google Gmail, 39

H

H&R Block, 244, 246, 273

Home Ownersite, 250-251

I

Identity theft, 25, 34, 41, 159, 192, 214-216, 218, 267

Investopedia.com, 200-201, 283

IRS, 80, 82, 84-85, 88, 92, 149, 159-160, 174, 236, 241-247, 262, 261, 265, 272, 283,

K

Kelly Blue Book, 257

Kiplinger, 149, 263, 272

Kiva, 175, 276

L

Lending Club, 175, 275

LendingTree, 171-172

M

Macintosh, 73

MasterCard, 163, 194

Medicare, 67, 152, 154-156, 233, 239, 271

Mergent Online, 198

Michelle Hooper, 212

Microsoft, 32, 42-44, 47, 62, 73, 75, 80, 110, 140-141, 276

Microsoft Excel, 110, 140

Microsoft Money, 32, 42-44, 80

Microsoft Office, 140, 276

Mint.com, 34, 42, 93, 135, 142, 145-146, 148, 202, 271

Moneybookers.com, 195

moneyStrands, 142

Morningstar, 148

MSN Hotmail, 39

MSN Money, 198

myFICO, 160, 266, 276

MyTotalMoneyMakeover.com, 144

N

National Foundation for Credit Counseling, 155, 277

O

OrganizeMyMoney.com, 144

P

P2P lending, 168, 172, 174-175

PaycheckCity.com, 237

PayPal, 112, 187, 194-196, 275

Paytrust, 127-128, 132

Peachtree, 47

Prosper, 175, 275

Q

Quick Collect, 115

Quicken, 31-32, 42-44, 47, 132-133, 139, 144, 172

Quicken Bill Pay, 132-133

R

RetailMeNot.com, 185, 273

Routing number, 97, 104, 113, 117, 129-130

RSS Feed, 264

S

SavingForCollege.com, 227

Schwab.com, 204

Scottrade.com, 201, 204

Search engine, 48, 50, 65, 83, 93, 186, 227, 243, 250, 267-268

Selling short, 207

ShareBuilder.com, 204

Smart Step, Inc., 148

SonicWALL, 62

Sony, 73, 277

Spending Diary, 146, 271

Stockscreen123, 198

Street name, 205

T

T+3, 207

TaxActOnline.com, 246

Tax-Compare.com, 247

TopTenREVIEWS, 42, 59, 61, 63, 272

Toshiba, 73, 277

Toys "R" Us, 163

TransUnion, 158, 160, 218, 276

TurboTax, 43, 245-246, 273

U

U.S. Postal Service, 15 99, 107, 132, 134, 167

USAA, 89, 117, 119, 152, 198

V

ValueLine, 198

Vanguard, 225

Virgin Money, 173-174, 275

Visa, 194

W

Wall Street, 201, 219, 263

Wall Street Journal, 219, 263

WeBidz, 190

WebRamp, 62

Wells Fargo, 109, 111

Wesabe, 93

Western Union, 114-115

Windows 7, 61, 63, 76

Windows Vista, 61, 63

Windows XP, 61-63, 65

Wire transfer, 105, 112-114

Y

Yahoo!, 32, 39, 48

Z

Zillow.com, 169, 259, 274

Zombie computer, 55